TRIUMPH
BOOKS

Barack Obama speaks at a rally in St. Louis on October 18, 2008. The crowd was estimated at 100,000 people.

This book is available in quantity at special discounts for your group
or organization. For further information, contact:

Triumph Books
542 South Dearborn Street
Suite 750
Chicago, Illinois 60605
(312) 939-3330
Fax (312) 663-3557

Printed in United States of America
ISBN: 978-1-60078-244-2

Content packaged by Mojo Media, Inc.
Joe Funk: Editor
Jason Hinman: Creative Director

For USA TODAY
Ken Paulson: Editor
Carol Stevens: Managing Editor/News
Richard Curtis: Managing Editor/Design
Phil Pruitt: Deputy Managing Editor/News
Lee Horwich: Senior Assignment Editor/Washington
Christy Hartsell: Director of Licensing
Ben Nussbaum: Book Editor

For ABC News
David Westin: President
Dave Davis: Executive Vice President
Derek Medina: Senior Vice President Business Affairs
John R. Green: Executive Producer Special
Programming and Development
Troy McMullen: Editorial Manager, 50 States in 50 Days series
Ida Mae Astute: Photo Editor
Brandon Lisy: Producer/ Editor

AP Images

Contents

Anchor, World News with Charles Gibson

Foreword by Charles Gibson

America from the Asphalt
A Journey Unlike Any Other

There is no standard playbook on how to cover an election. Watch the evening news or read the morning paper and you get the impression political journalists are most often tagging along with the candidates.

Well, there is a lot of that.

It entails hearing the stump speech over and over. Looking for any new emphasis in the same old words, trying to read meaning into an unguarded moment with the candidate, looking for the telltale expression that typifies what's happening with the campaign at a given time.

But just as important as listening to the candidates is listening to the voters. So often they have the most to say. And they "get" it. That's what is so heartening about covering an election year. You have the opportunity to talk to voters. And when they are as engaged as they have been since the very beginning of this campaign back in early 2007, it is a reminder of the vibrancy of our democracy—even after 232 years.

That's what was so exhilarating about the joint ABC News and USA TODAY project of visiting 50 states in 50 days.

None of us got to every state, but many of us got to travel to several states, view the election through a variety of prisms, and write about what we had seen.

It has become something of a cliché that this election or that one is "historic." But this time it was no cliché. For the first time we had an African American receive the nomination of a major political party. For the first time we had a woman come within a whisper of nomination. For the second time we had a female vice-presidential nominee. And we had a candidate who reminded the nation, that no matter how unpopular the Vietnam War may have been, there were great men and women who served the country most honorably in that conflict.

I was reminded as I watched the first presidential debate, which took place on the campus of the University of Mississippi, that it had been less than 50 years since that school was desegregated. And desegregation had not come without incident. Yet there was an African American on the campus of Ole Miss making the case that he should be president of the United States. And everyone at the school was excited that the debate was there. Remarkable.

In addition to traveling with our World News broadcast to a number of states during the primaries, I had the privilege of traveling in the Midwest for the "50 States

in 50 Days" project.

At a time of high gas and diesel prices, I was struck again, as we drove the interstates there, just how much American commerce in that part of the country moves by road—a good reminder for an easterner. At a time of high unemployment, I was reminded that a disproportionate share of the recent job losses have come in Midwest manufacturing...and I was also reminded just how stoic American workers can be. As the stock market tumbled, I was impressed by a retiree who said emphatically that he wouldn't consider selling his stocks. "Wouldn't be patriotic," he said. Some of the stock traders in New York would do well to listen to him.

Sitting atop a combine harvesting corn one afternoon with a farmer in Eldridge, Iowa, I heard his comments on U.S. trade policy that made far more sense than anything on that subject I heard while covering Congress for eight years. Talking to unemployed GM autoworkers in Dayton, Ohio, one night, I heard more optimism about job retraining and prospects for the future than I had heard in a couple of months from anyone on Wall Street. Seeing a set of

giant wind turbines in the middle of a field outside Bowling Green, Ohio, I got more excited about alternative energy than any reading on the subject could ever inspire.

The overall impression though was that it would be virtually impossible for John McCain to win. The sense that people just felt the government needed new direction was palpable. The extent to which they were investing hope in Barack Obama was manifest.

It is a great honor to travel the country with license to stop people and ask them what they're thinking about politically and how they see an election.

To that extent, I think all of us who traveled as part of the "50 States in 50 Days" project envy the candidates. Exhausting though it may be, that's what they do month after month—travel the country talking to voters.

But then they have to stop all the time and give those speeches. We journalists have no such obligation.

All of us are delighted to share our impressions of the country and of this past election. We hope you, the reader, come away the richer for sharing some of our journeys. ●

Editor, USA TODAY

Preface by Ken Paulson

Two decades later

Still "truly one nation"

At USA TODAY we'd been down this road before. Literally. Hitting the highways in partnership with ABC News was a great opportunity to talk to folks in their hometowns all across America. It also brought back some fond memories.

It was just over two decades ago that the then-young USA TODAY celebrated its fifth anniversary with a project called BusCapade, a trip to all 50 states on a bus that played state songs and was painted to resemble a USA TODAY newspaper vending machine. Subtle it wasn't.

The project was the brainchild of Al Neuharth, founder of USA TODAY, who recruited me from my job as editor of the *Green Bay Press-Gazette* to lead a team of journalists on this journey.

We ended up traveling 34,905 miles and interviewing more than 3,000 people. Our conclusion at the close of that trip: While every state had its own distinctive characteristics and qualities, there was a surprising amount of unity and a sense of being part of something bigger.

As Neuharth put it: "While our differences sometimes divide us, we are fundamentally a family united. The USA is truly one nation."

In 2008 we found a considerably different America. Much had changed in those last 21 years:

There were 242,804,000 of us then; today our population is more than 305 million. And we're far more diverse today, with racial and ethnic minorities now a third of our population, up from 23 percent in 1987.

The price of gasoline was 96 cents in 1987, a fraction of today's prices.

The Dow crossed the 2,000 mark for the first time in January 1987. Today it's in the 9,000 range, but wide swings continue.

But much more than the Dow and de-mographics have changed. There was no World Wide Web in 1987 and the pace of news and information has accelerated dramatically since then. We had cable TV, of course, but it wasn't overpopulated by pundits looking to score political points.

The phrase "red states and blue states" didn't even exist on that first trip across the country; it didn't come into vogue until the contested 2000 presidential election. We had our political differences, but we didn't color-code them.

That's not to suggest we didn't have our battles and controversies 21 years ago. But those divisions seem to have deepened, with less civility from every quarter.

It's no coincidence that both Barack Obama and John McCain made change the keynote of their campaigns. By any meas-ure, Americans wanted something different. But that doesn't necessarily mean they wanted something new.

Many would welcome the return of the spirit that has so often served this nation well, acknowledging our differences, but also celebrating what we share.

I saw that firsthand as the election cam-paign neared the end, and I stopped into my polling place right outside Nashville to participate in early voting. The line was long, but no one complained.

The mood was festive, with smiles and friendly conversation all around. A woman who suffered a stroke at 28, and who at 51 now leaned against a wall for support, said she had never waited so long to vote, but she clearly was happy to do it.

With our nation at a crossroads and facing unprecedented challenges at home and abroad, it felt good to vote our convic-tions and to truly have a say in the destiny of this nation and the future of our children. Patriotism trumps partisanship.

For all of our differences, we're still capable of being delighted by democracy, reveling in a nation in which every voice can be heard and every vote counts. And that shared love and respect for our most fundamental freedoms is in the end what makes us "truly one nation." ●

by Robin Roberts • Co-anchor, Good Morning America

Whistle-Stop America
Voices from the Train

The Good Morning America team—Chris Cuomo, Diane Sawyer, Robin Roberts, and Sam Champion—on the rear platform of the Whistle-Stop Tour '08 train that took them around the country.

I 'll tell you the truth—when the idea of doing Good Morning America for an entire week from a moving train first came up, my response was "what?" quickly followed by "how?"

I knew the "why." Our audience told us why, in emails, letters, postings on our Shout Out message board. They were hurting and, in this all-important election year, they needed our help in being heard. They were relying on us to listen and get them answers. That profound trust galvanized us and we all were eager to get going.

There were a few things we had to learn first. How do you pack for a train trip? No ball gowns, granted, but would it be cold, hot, or somewhere in-between? Would Diane Sawyer be able to get all the Diet Coke and Red Bull she needs to keep going? (Yes.) Would Sam Champion—in the gulf to cover Hurricane Ike—make it back for part of the trip? (Yes, thank goodness.) Will Chris Cuomo even fit in his sleeping berth? (No.) And would I be able to walk on a moving train? (Yes, thanks to our train attendant Sweet Lou Drummeter, who taught the whole GMA crew the "duck walk.")

And what would we do between stops? It turned out that spontaneous dance parties were popular (alas, the duck walk didn't help me here) and Sam and Chris had marathon Monopoly games, which they played by rules that the Parker Brothers would have frowned upon but left the rest of us rolling in the aisles.

Sweet Lou called "All aboard" on September 14, 2008, as GMA's Whistle-Stop Tour '08 pulled out of the station in Worcester, Massachusetts. Our first broadcast was from Stockbridge, Massachusetts, a beautiful, historic town nestled in the Berkshires. This is where Norman Rockwell painted our vision of the American dream, where small towns thrived and parents saw to it that their children's future was secure. We visited Joe's Diner in the nearby town of Lee, said by many to be the inspiration for Rockwell's famous painting of a boy and a policeman sitting at the counter. It's called "The Runaway," and we recreated

that moment with a local policeman and a little boy from town.

As we traveled west from Massachusetts to Niagara Falls, southwest along Lake Erie to Pennsylvania and Ohio, and then south to Maryland and West Virginia, finally pulling into Union Station in Washington, D.C., we saw two Americas from our train windows: the beautiful, ever-changing landscape, and the harsh reality facing the people living in towns along the tracks.

We saw the leaves turning in Massachusetts, a double rainbow over Niagara Falls, corn as far as the eye can see in Ohio, the Blue Ridge Mountains of West Virginia and the Capitol Dome, a beacon in the night sky.

Just as breathtaking was the landscape of faces greeting us along the way—cheerleaders, youth groups, families, and senior citizens, all sharing their smiles and their spirit. Their energy kept us going. They wanted us to love their hometowns as much as they do (and we did).

But another America greeted us, too: the America facing hard times. As the train rumbled on the tracks, the rumbling of trouble from Wall Street had begun, a crisis that was already part of the lives of the people we were about to meet.

In Massachusetts, Diane went doorknocking, going right up to people's homes to find out their concerns.

The cast of Good Morning America assembles outside Joe's Diner in Lee, Massachusetts during the joint ABC News/USA TODAY "50 States in 50 Days" initiative.

Frank Algerio said, "Health care. You know that's huge for me right now." Diane caught Richard Bonito just before he jumped in the shower. He's worried about energy costs, with a cold Northeastern winter on its way. For 30-year-old Nicky Vaughn, with friends in the service, it was the war, "it's time for us to leave, leave Iraq."

In the days that followed, the proud people of Rome, New York, once known as Copper City, expressed worry about jobs now that the factories have closed

down. In Niagara Falls, parents watched their children leave home for better opportunities as their Canadian neighbors thrive. And in Ohio, generations of the Lipps family have worked their farm but one of their sons, 13-year-old Jason, doesn't see himself following in the family tradition.

We heard heart-wrenching stories from people yearning for answers—

people who want to work, pay their bills, and make a better life for their children. We saw concern in their eyes.

There was pain in the eyes of Paul Camrye of Palmer, Massachusetts, the 89-year-old gentleman who shared his troubles, troubles he had kept secret from his family.

"We're suffering. We're suffering. I owe the oil bill from last year," he told me, as tears welled up in his eyes. "My taxes are not completely paid up. This never happened to me before, and I really don't know what I'm gonna do about it. It's just not…it's not the same life that I've always had."

This WWII veteran, who lived through the Great Depression, emotionally shared his hardship. Americans saw their grandfathers, their fathers and even themselves in his eyes. And even though they are facing

(above) Robin Roberts talks to Paul Camrye of Palmer, Massachusetts, an 89-year-old who shared troubles he had kept secret from his family until the interview. (below) All aboard for the "Whistle-Stop Train Tour" on Good Morning America

tough times themselves, Americans gave back.

Viewers called, they emailed, they demanded that we help them help Mr. Camrye. With the help of Catholic Charities of Atlanta, much-needed funds have been raised to help this lovely man attend to the bills that caused him so much worry. I returned to Palmer to visit Mr. Camrye a couple of weeks after our trip. He was beaming with gratitude and told me, "A smile improves your face value."

And that's when I realized that the two Americas—the country of beauty and the country of heartache—are inextricably linked. No matter where they're from or what troubles they're facing, Americans are bootstrappers and neighbors, able to find a way

through tough times together.

I had the privilege of introducing Linus Scott, 97 years young, to America. Mr. Scott was a Pullman Porter for 38 years, one of thousands of African American men, many of them recently freed slaves, who worked as attendants on the Pullman sleeping cars. They carried bags, served meals in the dining car, and answered passengers' every need, traveling on the train for weeks at a time, away from their families. Mr. Scott put four children through college and one through medical school on $68 a month plus tips. And yet, with so much at stake, Mr. Scott and his fellow porters were at the forefront of the civil rights movement, making sure their children would have greater opportunities.

And in Niagara Falls, we met young J.T. Robertson. This 12-year-old train enthusiast wanted to share his love of the rails with his friends, so he collected bottles and cans to buy tickets for those who couldn't afford to take a ride on his favorite local attraction, the Arcade & Attica steam train in Arcade, New York.

But he was devastated when he saw that physically challenged children couldn't ride the train because the 100-year-old equipment couldn't accommodate wheelchairs. J.T. wrote to Extreme Makeover: Home Edition for help. It was our great joy to introduce J.T. to the show's Ty Pennington, Michael Moloney, and Paige Hemmis, who helped make J.T.'s dream a reality. Now, the steam train is accessible to all, thanks to a young boy who wanted to share his passion.

We invited the candidates to stops along the Whistle-Stop Tour to convey your concerns, fears, disappointments, and hopes. We asked presidential candidates Senator Barack Obama and Senator John McCain your tough questions and pushed for the answers you needed. Senator Hillary Clinton climbed aboard to tell us how she would support the Democratic ticket.

Diane Sawyer interviews Senator Hillary Clinton on board the Whistle-Stop Tour '08 train.

And I think she would have accepted Diane's invitation to join the pajama party if there weren't 90 people sharing such close quarters.

And so, my thanks to you, who urged us to come to your hometowns, who got up very early in the morning to cheer us on, who shared your personal struggles and your triumphs, and who continue to give to others even when you're stretching to make ends meet. Traveling on the train, as Americans have for more than 170 years, the landscape just an arms-length away, and being able to shake your hands, give you hugs, and see your beautiful faces up close, reminded us all how blessed we are to be invited into your homes every morning. ●

By Jake Tapper • ABC News Senior Political/National Correspondent

ABC Contributors Jake Tapper

A Political Star is Born
Audacity and Hope

(above) Barack Obama serves birthday cake to ABC correspondent Jake Tapper, left, on his birthday while in flight Monday, August 4, 2008. (opposite) U.S. Senator Barack Obama, D-Ill., speaks to supporters after announcing his candidacy for president of the United States at the Old State Capitol in Springfield, Illinois on February 10, 2007.

I t was all there in Springfield, Illinois, that freezing Saturday morning in February 2007, both the promise and the improbability. Barack Obama, with just a touch over two years in the U.S. Senate under his belt, strode onto the stage and, with myriad allusions to Abraham Lincoln, declared his candidacy for the presidency.

No one sold Lincoln T-shirts, of course, when that 19th century president spoke at the Old State Capitol, whereas vendors offered various wares along those lines for Obama's big day—a hint of the Obama-mania that would soon capture the imagination of Iowa Democrats, young people, and other voters, not to mention far too many members of the media.

Behind the lectern, Obama's aides had hidden a heater for Obama, the better to project Kennedy-esque vigor from the chill. Hidden even further from public view was Obama's then-pastor, Rev. Jeremiah Wright, who had originally been scheduled to speak but instead was relegated to a private moment of family prayer, a nod to a recent magazine story that noted Wright's proclivity for radical statements.

Most jarring, of course, was the crowd.

Fifteen thousand had turned out to hear the junior senator. (That number now seems small, given Obama's ever-expanding crowds as his journey continued through Portland, Oregon, Berlin, Germany, and St. Louis, Missouri. But at the time it was quite impressive.) Bubbling with enthusiasm and optimism, the crowds told reporters how Obama had given them something to believe in. What that precisely was, of course, seemed vague. Obama would later acknowledge that many people projected onto him their desires for change, but he also artfully offered himself up as a projector.

The journey of Barack Hussein Obama Jr. from obscure Chicago pol to international phenomenon is no small accomplishment, and it was marked by an impeccable sense of timing, tough and savvy politics, charm, intellect, and not a little luck. He broke promises when it suited him—most glaringly his earlier pledge to enter into the public finance system. He obscured realities behind a veneer of eloquence. And yet he also in so many ways seemed the right person for this time. When he borrowed Dr. Martin Luther King's rhetoric about "the fierce urgency of now," it may have been self-

serving but it seemed, to many, compelling.

The reality of the fact that he might actually be able to pull this off began to sink in when he felled Senator Hillary Clinton in Iowa, helped by that state's anti-war left. It marked the start of the longest nomination race in modern history.

Winning the nomination was not the relatively easy feat of how Obama first won his senate seat in 2004—with two opponents withdrawing after divorce scandals followed by the inexplicable decision of the Illinois Republican Party to recruit the uncompromising conservative Alan Keyes, who had never lived in the state, as Obama's opponent. Obama would later acknowledge his "almost spooky good fortune" in that race.

No, there was nothing easy about Obama's presidential primary race. And there were serious bumps along the way— the intense and seemingly evanescent fight with Senator Hillary Clinton; Rev. Wright's

video-looped sermons and the beginning of questions about Obama's associates in Chicago's political swamp; serious questions about the preparedness to be commander-in-chief.

And while ultimately his victory over her was narrow, it was beyond question that even if he didn't out-work her he out-thought her.

His team organizationally was superb. When he started his campaign he told his senior staff that he had three rules: the campaign needed to be done at the grass roots level (ultimately more than $600 million dollars was raised from an unprecedented number of donors); no one could complain about anyone else to the media; and they needed to have fun. They accomplished all three tasks.

But beyond the fact that this relatively inexperienced public official with the exotic name somehow managed to defeat the powerful Clinton machine, become the first ever African American major party

presidential candidate, and launch such a promising journey to become the 44th president of the United States, was how he did it.

He did it by campaigning in red Republican states, Virginia and Indiana, North Carolina and Colorado, places Democratic nominees of far more obvious mainstream appeal had written off.

He faced challenges of his own making (an ill-conceived remark about small town economically distressed Pennsylvanians "cling"-ing to guns, God, and bigotry) and others that were not (the October economic crisis). But he seldom seemed distressed, and at all times he kept a consistent tone and message: the country needs change.

He was calling the nation to do something special, to come together for an important mission.

Whether there ultimately ends up being more to that task than the mere act of electing Barack Obama remains to be seen. ●

John McCain: Real American Hero

The Luckiest Guy in the World

Senator John McCain during an interview with ABC News in Ohio.

I first met John McCain in late October 2007. I introduced myself to him at a campaign event in Iowa. I explained that I had been covering Mitt Romney's campaign and was now assigned to his. He smiled mischievously. "Your reward will be in heaven," he said. I laughed. This was going to be fun, I sensed, even though I figured it wouldn't last long. McCain was trailing in the polls and practically broke. I gave him until late December, early January at best until he dropped out.

The differences between Romney's campaign and McCain's were a bit of a shock and a complete delight. The Romney campaign, like the candidate himself, was slick, sleek, disciplined and tightly controlled. McCain's was rollicking, loose, informal, ad hoc. Almost the only access to Romney was in a press conference. McCain was almost always accessible, either at one of the "gaggles"—the impromptu press availabilities that he held as many as three times a day—or aboard his campaign bus, the Straight Talk Express, where he held court sometimes for hours, fielding questions and commenting on anything and everything.

What I couldn't understand was how he could keep pushing his shoestring operation forward. It almost was embarrassing to witness, like watching someone singing off key at a concert.

But McCain had a plan—a long-shot one, but a plan—and he turned out to have luck. The plan was to concentrate on New Hampshire, whose January primary was the second contest in the long primary battle. Luck came in the form of Mike Huckabee, who became the hot new candidate in a crowded GOP field in which everyone seemed flawed in some way

The Hucka-boom, as it became known, succeeding in knocking off Romney in Iowa, setting up New Hampshire as McCain's first and last best chance to break out.

I went to dozens of town hall meetings in New Hampshire. In these free-wheeling sessions where anyone could stand up and ask him a question, he was engaging, charming, patient, and often very funny. It was the kind of old-fashioned retail politics that probably wouldn't have worked in a bigger state or one with a less idiosyncratic political tradition.

McCain won the New Hampshire primary. "The Mac is back," he proclaimed standing beside his bus.

I was invited several times to The Straight Talk, as the bus was nicknamed. I liked McCain. I could tell he wasn't as open or as casual as he pretended to be. His answers to political questions were often artful but dodgy. But it was casual and fun. The reporters loved it. McCain would crack wise, talk knowledgably about sports, about books, about history. He was very smart but not in an intellectual or showy way.

The McCain bandwagon began to roll. He lost Michigan, but won South Carolina, then Florida. He wracked up a string of key wins on Super Tuesday in March.

McCain was famously reluctant to talk about anything personal. But in interviews and in speeches, McCain would sometimes say, "Look, I am the luckiest guy in the world."

He would say it with such a fervor you knew it was genuine. But what did he mean, I wondered? That he was on his way to winning the GOP nomination against long odds? That he survived as a POW in Vietnam? That he'd had a long career in Congress? Was it an allusion to his family or friends or surviving a serious skin cancer? Or that he was affluent and comfortable thanks to his wife's wealth? All of that? Or something else that was significant and maybe known only to him?

With success, things changed gradually at first, but the pace of change soon increased.

We went to larger states where the bus was impractical. McCain got a plane in which he was physically removed from the press pack. He held fewer gaggles. His

answers were more carefully parsed.

In the spring, as the Democratic nomination battle went on and on, McCain seemed a bit at a loss of what to do. He did a "biography tour." He announced an economic plan. He went to Iraq and Europe. He held a lot of fundraisers.

In June, Obama emerged as his presumptive Democratic opponent. Under the sway of senior adviser Steve Schmidt, McCain became more and more inaccessible to the press that traveled with him. It was being done in the name of message discipline. It made sense tactically, but what was odd was McCain didn't seem at all regretful.

By now, McCain had Secret Service protection and there were no more gaggles. Formal press conferences even became rare. His campaign messages became more focused and harsh. We saw less and less of him. When we did, his face was often a mask.

By late summer, relations between McCain and the press had soured. McCain was wary, guarded, and distant.

He went six weeks at one point without holding a press conference, prompting one reporter to shout out as McCain boarded his bus after an event near Cleveland: "Is the Straight Talk Express now the No Talk Express?" McCain kept stepping.

The press became resentful. Some reporters were dismayed and disappointed that McCain was engaging in increasingly sharp, negative attacks on Obama. This was the guy who had pledged to run a "respectful" campaign. By the time the convention came and went, it seemed anything but respectful.

"It isn't beanbag," McCain liked to say about election politics. No, it isn't. But it hadn't always been that way.

We are left now with questions, perhaps unanswerable.

Did McCain change? Did he do what he believed he had to do because, well, that's

how the game—and it really is a kind of game—is played? Were we, the press, seasoned, cynical reporters we fancied ourselves, actually naive or even foolish to have ever thought the general election race with the most powerful office in the world on the line could be like January when McCain was still a long shot and it was a magical journey for all of us?

I will always remember the moment when McCain seemed happier than any other I ever saw.

It was the night he won the South Carolina primary in January. He had just vindicated his loss there in 2000 that had doomed that campaign and re-ignited his 2008 campaign.

McCain finished a live interview on the camera platform next to me. As he turned in my direction to leave, I leaned forward and said to him: "It's like the old saying, I guess, 'I've been rich and I've been poor and rich is better.'"

I don't know if McCain heard me over the din but he did something strange. McCain reached forward and started to embrace me. Then he caught himself—after all, I was a reporter, he was the candidate. We didn't embrace—and instead he shook my hand and thanked me. Then he climbed down from steps and was swallowed up by the cheering crowd. ●

By Cynthia McFadden • Co-anchor Nightline • Co-anchor Primetime

ABC Contributors | Cynthia McFadden

Going Home
Maine's Offshore Drilling Dilemma

Cynthia McFadden reporting from Maine, her home state, as part of the "50 States in 50 Days" series.

My home state of Maine is one of the poorest and coldest in the nation, and it is also mightily dependent on foreign oil. Eighty percent of the folks in Maine heat their homes with oil, which most of them are quickly becoming unable to afford. And so we wondered—as oil prices rose and offshore drilling got its own call to arms with "drill baby drill"—whether Maine is poised to look to offshore drilling to buck up its struggling economy?

My mother still lives in a log cabin on the coast of Maine. I called her before heading north. "Any talk up there about offshore drilling?" I asked, fresh from covering the Republican convention. "Not too much," she said. "You do know our Senator Susan Collins (R-ME) is for offshore drilling but against it here in Maine." That sounded promising.

Senator Collins was more than happy to explain her position: yes she thought that offshore drilling makes sense in places where the "people want it and there is an infrastructure to support it," but she noted, "That is not Maine." Maine's fishing industry depends on the fish-rich Georges Bank and anything that might mess with the Georges Bank (one of the seven most vibrant and important fishing areas in the world, by the way) was not getting an okay on her watch.

What did she think when she heard her fellow Republicans chanting "drill, baby, drill?" "I thought, that's not the whole answer, but the whole answer is more complicated than any quick slogan."

The president of the Gulf of Maine Research Institute, Don Perkins, agrees whole-heartedly. An independent scientific research center in Portland, the Gulf of Maine Institute doesn't take positions on issues, but its scientists study the ocean and the creatures that live in it. As for offshore drilling, Perkins said, no one is really sure how much oil and gas there is off the coast of Maine, or where it's located, and just trying to find out could have environmental consequences. "When you go looking for oil and gas you use seismic pulses and...there's been some indication that fish populations

scatter in the presence of that kind of intense sound activity." Perkins said he thought spending the day with a couple of Maine fishermen would help us understand how most Maine folks thought about drilling.

The next morning at 4:00 we found ourselves in Phippsburg, Maine, to rendezvous with Proctor Wells. Like his grandfather before him, Wells is a lobsterman. Fishing, he tells us, provides lots of time for thinking. And Proctor Wells has thought plenty about drilling. The price of diesel has made hauling his traps expensive. Wells explained he had to catch 100 lobsters to just break even. After four hours of continuous work, we'd brought in about 30. "It's not this bad everyday," he said. So you might think he'd want cheaper

diesel anyway he could get it. You'd be wrong. "If you want to drill on Georges Bank or here in the Gulf of Maine, to me, that doesn't make sense. You've got one of the few places on Earth that has got a huge potential to generate food."

But what about the impending heating oil crisis in Maine? Wells says his family is living it. His in-laws are faced with fuel bills this winter that will exceed their entire retirement income, including their social security. But still he says drilling won't solve the problem—certainly not in the short run—and might create a whole new set of environmental issues. Instead, he would like to see America more aggressively explore alternate energy resources. "I don't

Maine's fishing industry may come under even more pressure if the search for oil in its waters intensifies.

see any reason why we couldn't have, you know, hybrid boats. I think the smaller carbon footprint the better," he said.

He's disappointed with what he sees as "looking backward" at oil and not forward to alternatives. In fact, Susan Collins and other state leaders are encouraging scientists to explore new sources of energy. There is talk of harnessing Maine's record high tides and of placing wind farms far off the coast. Susan Collins says, Mainers want to help solve the energy crisis, just don't make them drill, baby. Don't. ●

Big River Banter
Down the Mighty Mississippi

David Muir's long cruise down the Mississippi River left him with a unique perspective and distinct impressions of America's heartland.

Our travels down the Mighty Mississippi brought us to small American cities, each rich with storied pasts, but each struggling with an uncertain future.

Our first stop was Quincy, Illinois, where Abraham Lincoln once fiercely debated Stephen Douglas during Lincoln's campaign to end slavery. So it was no surprise as we traveled through the Land of Lincoln that we found sharp political opinions and heartfelt hope that this presidential election would bring a better economic future.

Illinois far outpaces the unemployment rate of the nation. In the fall of 2008 there were six million workers in the state looking for employment. One of the workers we met was Bill Arnold, a single father of three whom we encountered at a barbeque cook-off on the banks of the Mississippi.

Hidden behind Arnold's beaming smile were the challenges he faces every day. Bill lost his job as a tool engineer when it was outsourced. Left looking for work, he decided to market the barbeque sauce that was already a culinary hit among family and friends. But Bill's fortune would be tested again when he learned he had brain cancer. During our afternoon with him, Bill told us of the treatment he'd undergone. And though his prognosis was uncertain, he remained the optimist, preferring to focus on the future for his three little girls.

As the smoke rose from his grill, his young daughters played the role of cheerleaders, watching their father compete in the contest that day. By late afternoon, there were blue ribbons for Bill. It was a moment of pride for a father who told me he hoped the next president would find ways to help struggling parents, budding business owners, and Americans who face the kind of medical hurdles he continues to tackle.

"You've got a single parent like me trying to struggle to make a business work. I don't ask for a handout from anybody," Bill told me. His story was one I kept close.

Another stop was in Helena, Arkansas. The struggling city of

7,000 may be small in size, but it was hardly lacking in pride.

On a brisk, late-summer evening, we found ourselves in the stands of the Helena–West Helena High School for the first football game of the season. Though a fiercely contested presidential election was nearing and a national economic crisis was playing out on the front page of daily newspapers, you wouldn't have known it that night.

The team's star, Darius Winston, Arkansas' top high school football prospect, had announced he was staying close to home. Weighing countless offers, Winston chose to play for his home state at the University of Arkansas. It was a welcome piece of good news for this challenged city.

Helena has not recovered from the loss of a tire manufacturer several years ago and the state of Arkansas lost another 6,000 manufacturing jobs in 2008.

Though Darius has a bright future, his mother told me she knows other parents in Helena worry about the future for their own children.

"People are struggling to pay for the simple things like a meal for their kids. You're having to pay for gas prices. That's a struggle they face everyday," Debra West said.

They are the kind of struggles that some political analysts said put the typically red state of Arkansas in play this election. The same voters who elected Bill Clinton and Mike Huckabee as governors once again showed their political range.

We spent the day with Tate and Ashley Olinghouse of Little Rock. Cradling their 10-week-old boy in their arms, they joked

David Muir reports from the Mississippi River in Helena, Arkansas, as part of the "50 States in 50 Days" coverage leading up to the presidential election.

about how their little boy will vote one day after being raised in a home where Mom and Dad disagree. Both told me the economy was the number-one issue, but both offered differing views on which candidate would be better suited to fix it.

"We are in a time that we don't need to be rolling the dice and choosing somebody that's untested and unproven," Ashley said.

Her husband quickly responded, "But isn't the question, how's the last eight years, how's that worked for us?"

Theirs was a debate echoed in homes across this country that will ultimately decide who our next president will be. ●

By Dan Harris • Anchor, World News Sunday

Election Recollections
Portraits from the West

Republican Dino Rossi, the challenger to Washington Governor Chris Gregoire, a Democrat, takes part in their final debate on October 15, 2008, in Seattle.

Quite rightly, most of the attention during the election was focused on McCain and Obama. Down the ticket, however, in states all over the country, there was a rich pageant of characters. On a swing through Oregon, Washington and California, I spent time with some of them.

1. Is this candidate trying to hide that he's a Republican?

It wasn't easy for Dino Rossi being a Republican running for governor in the very blue state of Washington.

How blue? On a brief visit, I saw bumper stickers saying, "Republicans for Obama." At a costume store in Seattle, they were doing a brisk business in Sarah Palin Halloween masks—often paired with devil horns.

So it was no wonder, said critics, that Rossi decided not to list himself as a Republican on his campaign signs or even on the ballot. Instead, he went with "GOP," the acronym for the party's long-standing nickname, "Grand Old Party."

When I interviewed Rossi after a campaign event at a country club outside of Tacoma, he repeatedly insisted that he had always campaigned this way—and that it was not a way to dodge a damaged brand.

"That's sheer silliness," he told me. "Every speech I give I talk about me being a Republican. That's no secret. I mean everybody in our state knows that I'm a Republican."

However, his Democratic opponent, Governor Christine Gregoire (who beat Rossi by just 133 votes in 2004) wasn't buying it.

"Oh he's clearly hiding from the label of Republican, no question about it," she told me. "Everywhere he goes he identifies himself as GOP. He's hiding from all of the policies of the Bush administration despite the fact that he supported them all."

The Democrats unsuccessfully took Rossi to court to try to force him to put "Republican" instead of "GOP" on the ballot. They argued that polling showed even many Republicans didn't know what GOP meant.

The whole donnybrook was an interesting illustration of what a tough year 2008 was for Republicans across the country, after eight years of George W. Bush.

In neighboring Oregon, also a blue state, Senator Gordon Smith ran campaign ads linking himself to Barack Obama—and even Massachusetts Senators Ted Kennedy and John Kerry.

Speaking of Oregon...

2. The most controversial man in Oregon?

With his business casual attire and slightly shaggy hair, Bill Sizemore looks like a regular guy. But he is the focus of a multi-million dollar campaign of negative attack ads—and he's not even a politician.

Sizemore is what's called a "ballot-ician." Over the past 14 years, the former business-man has filed more than a hundred ballot initiatives, on everything from property taxes to education to home construction.

As he showed me stacks of paper con-taining rows of petition signatures neatly piled up on his desk, I asked him, "Do you sit around the house and dream this stuff up and then write it?"

"Yes," he said. "That's how it happens."

Sizemore had five initiatives on the ballot during the election, including one that would lower state taxes, one that would give merit pay to teachers, and one that would allow homeowners to do $35,000 worth of renovations to their homes without getting a permit.

"I have strong convictions about basic is-sues," he told me. "Things like property rights, lower taxes. I think issues like that are moral issues."

In his attempt to change Oregon's laws, however, Sizemore—who's a self-described conservative—has made a powerful and di-verse coalition of enemies. Their basic argu-ment is that Sizemore's initiatives may sound good at first glance, but are usually so vaguely worded and ill-conceived that they would have enormously negative consequences.

This year, as they do every year, Size-more's opponents—lead by the state public employee unions—mounted a multimillion dollar campaign against Sizemore's initia-

tives, including television ads and an anti-Sizemore website.

Members of the Oregon teachers' union told us Sizemore's education initiatives would hurt students.

"He has no experience in education," said public school teacher Jen Murray. "He writes these initiatives where he doesn't have to deal with the consequences. Whereas all Oregonians in public school will."

Sizemore's critics say he's motivated not only by his conservative philosophy, but also by money.

"I think the reason he does it is because it's a way to make a living," said Larry Wolf of the Oregon Education Association.

Critics say Sizemore has turned the ini-tiative system, designed as a populist tool, into a profit-making enterprise. Sizemore denies this. He says he only makes about $100,000 per year and that, more impor-tantly, he is using the system exactly as it was meant to be used.

As he told me, "What we use the initia-tives to do is to put initiatives on the ballot that have broad popular support that the legislature would refuse to deal with. And the fact that I do it for a living is irrelevant to the thing itself."

Being a ballot-ician has not been an easy road for Sizemore. He's had a very low success rate on his initiatives. He's been suc-cessfully sued by the unions for filing false signatures. And of course he and his family have had to endure a tsunami of attack ads.

3. Should Jan and Bonny be allowed to stay married?

On a sunny October day in San Diego, Jan Garbowski and Bonny Russell walked me down the aisle of their church, re-enacting for me their wedding day. The two women had been married just weeks early. Tears welled up in their eyes as they told the story.

"It was a very incredible day," said

Bonny. "We thought after being together 20 years we would never see the day that we would marry."

Bonny and Jan were one of hundreds of lesbian and gay couples to marry after the California State Supreme Court legalized gay marriage in the Spring of 2008.

But then a coalition of social conserva-tives gathered enough signatures for Proposition 8, a measure to enact a consti-tutional amendment against gay marriage—which provoked Bonny and Jan to go public with their story.

"We love each other," said Jan, "and to take away our rights or the rights of any-body else in our position or who falls in love on November 5 is just so wrong and against what I believe as a person of faith."

Just a few miles away, in a small room on the top floor of an evangelical church, sev-eral dozen young Christians from around the nation were engaged in a 40-day, nonstop session of fasting and praying. They were praying for the passage of Proposition 8.

"We believe it's a defining moment in American history," said Lou Engel, the organizer of the event. "Stakes are real high. As California goes so goes the whole nation. And in many ways California is a leadership state for not just America but the whole world."

The Yes on 8 campaign received millions of dollars from religious conservatives—including Christians, Mormons, and Jews—from across the state and the nation. The No forces raised money from celebrities, including Brad Pitt and Steven Spielberg.

"We live in a democracy not a theoc-racy," said Jan Garbowski. "I certainly respect everyone to practice their faith and hold fast to their faith but I'm just amazed that anybody of faith would take away somebody else's rights. It's amazing to me and I don't understand it." ●

by Kate Snow • Anchor, Good Morning America Weekend

ABC Contributors | Kate Snow

American Impressions
The Landscapes of an Election and a Nation

Kate Snow reporting from the Badlands National Park in South Dakota.

The road to Hanging Rock, Ohio, winds along the scenic Ohio River in the far southern part of the state, just across the border from Kentucky. The town of 279 people is perched on a cliff—and it looks to an outsider like it might just be clinging on for dear life.

I visited Hanging Rock in February 2008 with Senator Hillary Clinton. We listened as a middle-aged woman broke down, telling the senator her family was barely making it on less than twenty thousand dollars a year. One quarter of the voters in Lawrence County, where Hanging Rock is located, live below the poverty line.

It was one of those moments that forced you to take a deep breath and look around, to reflect on your surroundings.

There were times during the long election year of 2008 when I barely knew where I was when I awoke in the morning. More than once I had to check the hotel notepad next to my bed to see what state I was in.

But now that I've had time to reflect back, I realize what an amazing journey it was.

I traveled through more than half of our nation's 50 states over the year—from a blinding white-out snowstorm near Fort Madison, Iowa, in early January to sunrise over the cattle yards in Fort Worth, Texas, in March to a vivid valley of orange-and-red maples outside Scranton, Pennsylvania, in late October. Through all those travels, what was most striking was the diversity of the geography of this enormous country. Every day brought a new, entirely different landscape.

Where else but Saint Louis would I find a manmade arch that so captures the ambition of a nation, its westward expansion?

Where else but South Dakota would I see the majesty of Mount Rushmore and then discover a lunar terrain like I had never seen before in the Badlands?

Where else but Alaska would I be able to look out from the window of a float plane and see the magenta hues of sunset splayed

across jagged peaks, the Homer spit down below us?

Like the peaks and valleys I saw from that plane, there were ups and downs throughout the 2008 campaign. (Just ask Senator Clinton, she'll tell you.) In the primary months, the race seemed to change shape as quickly as the scenery outside my window did.

But there was also a constant. No matter where I went, no matter what part of the country—from Mary Anne's Diner in Derry, New Hampshire, to Lynn's Paradise Cafe in Louisville, Kentucky—I discovered that people were incredibly engaged in the election.

In Milwaukee, Wisconsin, Kathie Beuscher told me as she left the primary polling place: "The opportunity to really have my voice heard was important to me."

"It's nice to have a voice," Beth Payne said thousands of miles away, in Fort Worth.

I think most Americans felt that way. Whatever their politics, they wanted to be heard.

And whether they hailed from a dirt-road-accessible town outside of Anchorage or a swanky suburb of San Diego, voters told us—over and over again—that they felt like a part of something bigger.

There is something awe-inspiring about looking out over a gorgeous vista. I was lucky enough to see a lot of them in 2008: the Berkshire Mountains of Massachusetts, the White Mountains of New Hampshire, and Alaska's Kenai peninsula, to name just a few.

It was humbling, even breathtaking.

But it was equally inspiring to realize that the people who live in those places,

From east to west, Americans proved themselves incredibly engaged in this election that promises to reshape the political landscape.

and in each and every state I visited, were all motivated by much the same thing.

Out on the road you discover the American spirit.

It was embodied in the guy at the gas station in Drake's Branch, Virginia, who showed us the way back to the interstate when we were hopelessly lost. Or the man who stopped to pull us out of a ditch in Kent, Ohio.

And like that woman in Hanging Rock, what everyone was searching for was a brighter future...so they can enjoy all those beautiful sunrises. ●

A stately home sits in disrepair in Epes, Alabama, on June 2, 2008. Epes is a small town in Sumter County, which has seen little growth in the last two decades.

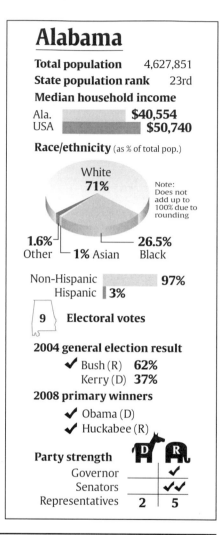

Alabama

Total population   4,627,851

State population rank   23rd

Median household income

Ala.	**$40,554**
USA	**$50,740**

Race/ethnicity (as % of total pop.)

White **71%**

Note: Does not add up to 100% due to rounding

1.6% Other — **1%** Asian   **26.5%** Black

Non-Hispanic **97%**
Hispanic **3%**

9   **Electoral votes**

2004 general election result
✔ Bush (R) **62%**
   Kerry (D) **37%**

2008 primary winners
✔ Obama (D)
✔ Huckabee (R)

Party strength

	D	R
Governor		✔
Senators		✔✔
Representatives	2	5

South's rural towns shrink as economic troubles grow

Decline in family farms, a lack of jobs causing heavy population losses

By Larry Copeland • Excerpt from Tuesday, June 17, 2008 • GAINESVILLE

This speck-on-the-map town, once Alabama's third largest, is home to fewer than 400 hardy souls. This is life in a vanishing place: Sumter County, Ala., one of the nation's fastest-shrinking counties. Since 2000, the population of the county has declined 10.1%, according to the Census Bureau.

Here in the Southeast, demographics have been dominated by dynamic growth. But there's another story here—Sumter and most of the Southeast's other shrinking counties are in the so-called Black Belt, where vestiges of the Old South—de facto school segregation, poor race relations and entrenched poverty—are most prevalent. Rural towns in the Southeastern states are hollowing out.

The Black Belt, which stretches from Virginia to East Texas, is named for the rich, dark topsoil that drew plantation owners to the region. Today the term also refers to the region's large African-American population, many descended from slaves brought to work on the plantations. Commonly defined as 623 mostly contiguous counties across 11 states, the Black Belt is home to about 40% of the nation's 40 million blacks.

"In the Black Belt, African-Americans in large numbers began migrating north to relatively lucrative factory jobs at the beginning of the 20th century," says professor Joe Sumners, director of the Economic and Community Development Institute at Auburn University. The small-farm econ-omy of the region was dying out and the businesses that had supported small farming—cotton gins, grain distributors, equipment sales—dried up.

Sumners and others are pinning hopes on a new economic development deal. Gov. Bob Riley and U.S. Steel Corp. announced in April that the company will build a steel plant here that eventually will create 235 jobs and bring a $450 million total economic impact.

The plant also will create secondary jobs and generate other openings as people move to jobs there, says professor Ken Tucker, dean of the business school at University of West Alabama. It "has the potential to transform this area," he says. ●

Voters in Arkansas aren't just concerned about the national issues like the economy and war in Iraq—they are also worried about local economic pressures.

Arkansas

Total population   2,834,797

State population rank   32nd

Median household income

Ark.	**$38,134**
USA	**$50,740**

Race/ethnicity (as % of total pop.)

White **80.9%**

2.2% Other

1.1% Asian

15.8% Black

Non-Hispanic **95%**

Hispanic **5%**

6   **Electoral votes**

2004 general election result

✔ Bush (R)   **54%**

✔ Kerry (D)   **45%**

2008 primary winners

✔ Clinton (D)

✔ Huckabee (R)

Party strength

	D	R
Governor	✔	
Senators	✔✔	
Representatives	3	1

Local matters share ballot spotlight in Ark.

Voters will weigh issues from sales tax to proposed lottery

By Joanne Bratton • Excerpt from Thursday, September 25, 2008 • MOUNTAIN HOME

Voters will be thinking about the economy, the Iraq war and health care when they go to the polls Nov. 4. But in Mountain Home, they'll also be thinking about a proposed hike in the 8% sales tax to pay for an indoor swimming pool in Cooper Park.

The pool's a big topic in this small Ozarks city of 11,000. It's an example of how national issues can influence local concerns.

Some residents, such as Howard Richert, 70, say they're not willing to pay extra and feel the addition to the city's outdoor pool is a luxury in difficult times.

"Too many people are living day-to-day," Richert said. "It's hard enough to pay for groceries. It's nice to have all this stuff if the economy was different."

Then there are the people on the other side. Linda Vornheder, 64, wants the pool and is willing to pay the higher tax. "People with chronic illnesses, like arthritis, will benefit from the low-impact exercise," she said.

While Mountain Home residents talk about the pool and other local issues, they're also eager to see how the next president will handle the big picture.

"The bottom line is the economy and the war," said resident Tom Fazio, 66, whose son fought in Iraq for 15 months. "Everybody's getting tired of higher prices."

Local Republicans say McCain has the experience to lead the country and were pleasantly surprised by his choice of run-

ning mate, Sarah Palin.

"I think it's a powerhouse ticket," said Baxter County Republican Committee Chairman Gary Smith, 53, of Lakeview.

Those who plan to vote for Obama say they agree with his stance on the environment, health care and public policy that affects families.

"Sen. Barack Obama and Joe Biden are willing to roll up their sleeves and try to get something started to solve the energy problem," said Nell Engeler, 70, president of the Arkansas Federation of Democratic Women's Baxter County Chapter. ●

Wall Street waves unsettle Connecticut

Voters' desire for change aids Obama

By Charisse Jones • Excerpt from Monday, October 6, 2008 • GREENWICH

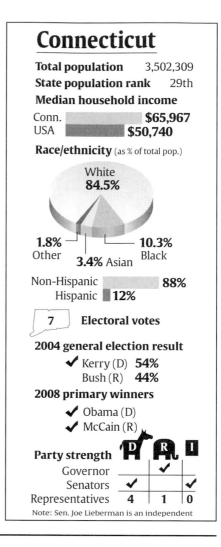

In downtown Greenwich, Connecticut: Wall State's woes are magnified in this state, where many financial services workers live.

Connecticut

Total population   3,502,309
State population rank   29th
Median household income
Conn.   **$65,967**
USA   **$50,740**
Race/ethnicity (as % of total pop.)

White **84.5%**

1.8% Other   **3.4%** Asian   **10.3%** Black

Non-Hispanic **88%**
Hispanic **12%**

7   **Electoral votes**

2004 general election result
✔ Kerry (D) **54%**
   Bush (R) **44%**

2008 primary winners
✔ Obama (D)
✔ McCain (R)

Party strength	**D**	**R**	**I**
Governor		✔	
Senators	✔		✔
Representatives	4	1	0

Note: Sen. Joe Lieberman is an independent

Despite appearances, the worries of Main Street are being felt even here, in Wall Street's well-manicured backyard.

"I'm old and coming up to retirement," says Jeff Ramer, 64, an attorney who has lived more than half his life in this affluent community. "I'm concerned that the money we put aside for retirement has taken a great hit."

Through the years, he has voted for more Republicans than Democrats, he says. But the financial crisis roiling Wall Street has solidified his desire for political change — and his support for Democratic presidential nominee Barack Obama. "It has a bear-

ing for me," Ramer says of the economy.

The meltdown that has caused investment firms to fall, stocks to plunge and the credit markets to slow to a virtual standstill has made the economy the primary concern for many Americans as they prepare to select a new president in barely four weeks.

The tremors on Wall Street and fallout from the $700 billion rescue plan President Bush signed into law on Friday are felt acutely in this state. It is home to numerous hedge funds, Fortune 500 companies and residents who work in finance and related industries on Wall Street and elsewhere.

Connecticut draws 45% of its income tax revenue from Fairfield County, a finance center next door to New York City. Greenwich alone, tucked in the county's southern end, paid more than $598 million in state income taxes in 2006, 12.7% of the statewide total, according to the governor's office.

Though the state has more unaffiliated voters than those who declare themselves Republican or Democrat, polls show Connecticut solidly in Obama's column. In a SurveyUSA poll taken Sept. 24-25 for New York's WABC-TV, 54% of those questioned support Obama, and 38% prefer Republican John McCain. ●

Shipwreck Beach in Poipu on Kauai's south shore, where a raft of new resort and real estate developments are stirring controversy.

Hawaii

Total population   1,283,388
State population rank   42nd
Median household income

Hawaii	**$63,746**
USA	**$50,740**

Race/ethnicity (as % of total pop.)

- Asian **39.9%**
- **2.9%** Black
- **29.1%** White
- **28.1%** Other

Non-Hispanic	**92%**
Hispanic	**8%**

4   **Electoral votes**

2004 general election result
✔ Kerry (D) **54%**
Bush (R) **45%**

2008 primary winners
✔ Obama (D)
✔ McCain (R)

Party strength

	D	R
Governor		✔
Senators	✔✔	
Representatives	2	0

Economic ebb tide hits Hawaii's tourism

Obama expected to win home state

By Dan Nakaso • Excerpt from Monday, October 20, 2008 • HONOLULU

The nation's economic woes are hitting Hawaii's tourism industry hard. Even before the economy reached the current crisis level, the Hawaii Department of Business, Economic Development and Tourism estimated in August that the number of visitors would decline by more than half a million this year, from a 2007 peak of 7.63 million to 7.12 million. It also forecast that visitors, who spent $12.81 billion in the state in 2007, would spend $11.99 billion in 2008.

Matters worsened in September, when the agency reported a 24.2% drop in tourists from August 2007. That decline was the largest year-over-year drop ever, says Marsha Wienert, Hawaii's tourism liaison. "Hawaii's economy is reliant on tourism, and the largest source of tourists to the islands is the U.S. mainland," Wienert says. "When there's a downturn in the economy on the U.S. mainland, it affects Hawaii's tourism."

Officials and residents are divided over whether Democratic presidential nominee Barack Obama, who was born in Honolulu, or Republican counterpart John McCain would be most effective at addressing the decline.

"Either candidate is going to have to focus on this economic crisis, to rein in oil prices and increase the value of our dollar and how Hawaii relates to the world's markets," says state Rep. Ryan Yamane, a Democrat who is chairman of Hawaii's House Tourism and Culture Committee. "That economic engine has got to be a focus, which will directly relate to tourism."

"Sen. McCain provides the assurance that our military will remain strong," says Andy Blom, executive director for the Hawaii McCain campaign. "He will ease our tax burden, which not only helps us in our pockets but helps us dramatically in tourism."

"As the economy goes, so goes tourism," said Brian Schatz, head of the Hawaii Democratic Party. "Sen. McCain's economic policies are indistinguishable from President Bush's. Sen. Obama's presidency will put us back on a path to economic recovery, and that will help our No. 1 industry." ●

Bob Bowman and many Iowans want to make sure the next president supports ethanol production.

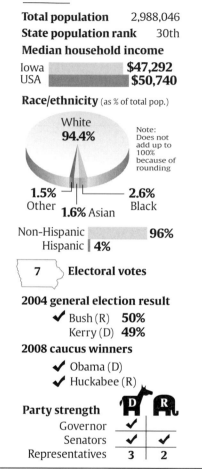

Iowa

Total population   2,988,046
State population rank   30th
Median household income

Iowa	**$47,292**
USA	**$50,740**

Race/ethnicity (as % of total pop.)

White **94.4%**

Note: Does not add up to 100% because of rounding

1.5% Other   **1.6%** Asian   **2.6%** Black

Non-Hispanic **96%**
Hispanic **4%**

7   **Electoral votes**

2004 general election result
✔ Bush (R)   **50%**
   Kerry (D)   **49%**

2008 caucus winners
✔ Obama (D)
✔ Huckabee (R)

Party strength   **D**   **R**

	D	R
Governor	✔	
Senators	✔	✔
Representatives	3	2

Tight race in Iowa could make ethanol a key issue

Candidates' views on biofuels may sway undecideds

By Grant Schulte • Excerpt from Friday, October 10, 2008 • DES MOINES

There are many things Bob Bowman will consider when he casts a ballot in this year's presidential race.

The 58-year-old eastern Iowa farmer wants a strong free-trade advocate in the White House. He wants a president who strengthens the financial safety net for farmers. And, like many Iowans, Bowman wants a proven supporter of ethanol.

"Obviously, that's toward the top of the list," says Bowman, who leans Republican but says his vote is "still up for grabs."

Bowman, who farms 2,000 acres, illustrates what agricultural and political experts such as Iowa State University political scientist Steffen Schmidt say is a potential lever to sway on-the-fence voters in Iowa.

Ethanol might have slipped off the na-

tional radar, he says, but could grow in importance if the race in Iowa tightens between Republican John McCain and Democrat Barack Obama.

"I think it's always going to weigh in with a certain segment of voters who see ethanol as an important source of alternative energy," Schmidt says.

Both campaigns insist their approach to biofuels would better serve Iowans and the nation.

McCain supports energy alternatives such as ethanol, but he believes the fuel additive can compete without "isolationist tariffs and special interest subsidies," Iowa campaign spokeswoman Wendy Riemann says.

Jenni Lee, an Iowa spokeswoman for Obama, says Obama's experience repre-

senting Illinois has positioned him as an authority on ethanol's benefits.

"While Sen. Obama is committed to supporting Iowa biofuels, Sen. McCain sides with oil companies over ethanol," Lee said in an e-mail.

Iowa leads the nation's biofuel output, providing 31% of all U.S. ethanol with 28 refineries, according to a January report by John Urbanchuk, director of LECG, a financial analysis firm. Iowa has 14 ethanol plants under construction, which will boost production by nearly 70%, the report states.

In Iowa, ethanol also generated $2.9 billion in household income in 2007, generated more than 96,000 jobs since its creation and increased the gross domestic product by 10%, the report says. ●

"He touches all of us": Andre Bishop, a fan of Barack Obama, chats at a news-stand in Chicago's Washington Park neighborhood.

Illinois

Total population 12,852,548
State population rank 5th
Median household income

Ill.	**$54,124**
USA	**$50,740**

Race/ethnicity (as % of total pop.)

White **79.2%**

1.5% Other
4.3% Asian
15.0% Black

| Non-Hispanic | **85%** |
| Hispanic | **15%** |

21 Electoral votes

2004 general election result
✔ Kerry (D) **55%**
Bush (R) **44%**

2008 primary winners
✔ Obama (D)
✔ McCain (R)

Party strength

	D	R
Governor	✔	
Senators	✔ ✔	
Representatives	11	8

Illinois places big expectations on Obama

But some say former cynics have now set bar too high

By Judy Keen • Excerpt from Wednesday, September 24, 2008 • CHICAGO

Catherine Haskins is 36 and has never bothered to vote in a presidential election. She says that will change Nov. 4 when she votes for Barack Obama.

Until now, Haskins, a single mom and small business owner in Washington Park, one of this city's poorest neighborhoods and just a few blocks from Obama's Hyde Park home, never believed that any presidential candidate could make a difference in her life or the lives of her three sons.

In Obama, she says, she sees a politician who was raised by his own single mom and by his grandparents, a former community organizer who worked in Chicago neighborhoods much like her own. "He gets it. He's lived it," she says.

Illinois, which sent Obama to the U.S. Senate in 2004 with 70% of the vote, could help elect the USA's first African-American president. That prospect has prompted some people here to set aside cynical attitudes about politicians, says Haskins. "I just know that he's going to make things better for people like me," she says.

Paul Green, a political science professor at Chicago's Roosevelt University, worries that people in Washington Park expect more from Obama than he can deliver—even from the Oval Office.

The community's problems are "the same old story: jobs, education, drugs," he says. "Change is not going to be done by a president. It's not going to be done by waving a wand."

People invested the same expectations in Harold Washington, a Democrat, when he became Chicago's first black mayor in 1983, Green says, and "nothing changed."

Retiree Marilyn Nash, 61, says she understands why people think Obama can improve lives here, but she isn't sure he can fulfill those hopes. "Our problems are deep and old," she says. "We need better-paying jobs, better housing, real stuff. Politicians, even Barack, mostly give us words. That's not enough."

Yet Haskins sees in Obama "the beginning of something new" here and across the country. "He's not disconnected from poor and struggling people." ●

Jewelry store owner Louise Walker, left, talks with employee Autumn Garfield, 21, in Bismarck, N.D. Walker is voting for Republican McCain, Garfield is undecided.

North Dakota

Total population	639,715
State population rank	48th

Median household income

N.D.	**$43,753**
USA	**$50,740**

Race/ethnicity (as % of total pop.)

White **91.6%**

6.6% Other   **0.8%** Asian   **1%** Black

Non-Hispanic **98%**
Hispanic **2%**

3 Electoral votes

2004 general election result
✔ Bush (R)   **63%**
Kerry (D)   **35%**

2008 caucus winners
✔ Obama (D)
✔ Romney (R)

Party strength

	D	R
Governor		✔
Senators	✔✔	
Representatives	1	0

Usually red state, N.D. not 100% sold on McCain

Voters wary of senator's link to Bush and votes against farm bill, ethanol

By Andrea Stone • Excerpt from Tuesday, September 30, 2008 • MINOT

At 19, Megan Walser is undecided who will get her first vote for president. Rising costs of gas, food, rent and tuition are on her mind. As the daughter of a rancher in Rhame, she's thinking about farm issues, too.

But what may have caught her eye most this presidential season was who made time to campaign in North Dakota.

"I was surprised to see (Democrat Barack) Obama in Fargo," she says. "We're kind of like a forgotten state."

Not this year. North Dakota hasn't voted for a Democrat for president since Lyndon Johnson in 1964, but observers across the political spectrum here say it's too soon to color the state red in November.

"This is a surprisingly tight race. It's still leaning Republican, but what's different is it's usually a lock," says Steve Light, a political scientist at the University of North Dakota in Grand Forks.

"I was raised Republican, but I vote for the person, not the party," says Pam Hopkins, 57, a college bookstore manager.

Even staunch Republicans "are looking for something different than the last eight years," says Holmberg, 63.

North Dakotans are split evenly over the Iraq war. Light says regional issues may prove more decisive.

McCain "has some baggage," Holmberg says. Among the heaviest: Senate votes against the farm bill, ethanol subsidies and

tax credits for wind energy.

"We're sitting on it, and it's blowing over our heads," says Beth Kjelson, 54, who co-owns a Minot art supply store. The Democrat supports Obama's priority on tapping renewable energy sources rather than McCain's emphasis on increasing offshore oil drilling.

In a state where triple-digit commutes are common, voters want a candidate who can bring relief at the gas pump. "I drive 125 miles a day," says Democratic state Sen. Joel Heitkamp, who commutes between his Hankinson home and Fargo office. "We have no choice but to drive, so $4 gas gets everybody's attention." ●

Zach Conway pulls the hose away from his tanker truck on the lot of the Nebraska - Iowa Supply Company, in Omaha. Though traditionally a red state, many Nebraskans say the vote is up for grabs.

Nebraska

Total population	1,774,571
State population rank	38th

Median household income

Neb.	**$47,085**
USA	**$50,740**

Race/ethnicity (as % of total pop.)

White
91.6%

2.3% Other
1.7% Asian
4.4% Black

Non-Hispanic **92%**
Hispanic **8%**

5 Electoral votes

2004 general election result

✔ Bush (R) **66%**
✔ Kerry (D) **33%**

2008 primary winners[1]

✔ Obama (D)
✔ McCain (R)

1 - Democrats held state caucuses and a primary, Obama won both

Party strength

	D	R
Governor		✔
Senators	✔	✔
Representatives	0	3

Typically red Nebraska can split electoral votes

State part of an "algebraic equation" to the presidency

By Andrea Stone • Excerpt from Friday, October 17, 2008 • OMAHA

"We're the campaign working hardest," says Ralph Morocco, a "retired Republican" volunteer for Barack Obama, and a health care consultant. "I don't know if hard work always pays off."

A law that allows the state's five Electoral College votes to be split up has encouraged Democrats to try for one of them. "The campaigns of old used to be a basic mathematic formula...to get to 270," says John Berge, Obama's state director. "Today's campaign is more of an algebraic equation."

Nebraska and Maine are the only two states that don't have winner-take-all rules for electoral votes. In those states, the can-didate who wins a majority statewide gets two votes. The other votes are awarded to the winner in each congressional district.

Neither state has ever split votes, but Democrats say Nebraska's 2nd District, which includes most of Omaha and part of Sarpy County, may be within reach.

The Illinois senator has 15 paid staffers in Omaha. Bill Clinton had two in 1992, the first election under proportional voting.

"Nebraska pretty much never mattered," Democratic activist Judy Monaghan says. "We've never had this kind of activity."

Randall Atkins, a political scientist at the University of Nebraska at Omaha, says Obama has generated more enthusiasm among Democrats than Al Gore and John Kerry combined. "The fact you put feet on the ground in Omaha is a big deal," he says.

Republican City Councilman Jim Vokal says his party is mobilizing voters in Sarpy County. Home to Offutt Air Force Base, it is filled with retired members of the military who like McCain and social conservatives excited about his running mate, Alaska Gov. Sarah Palin.

"This has united the party," Vokal says. "We're now excited about the ticket."

Independent Lucas Munderloh, 26, a University of Nebraska student, will "probably" vote for Obama but knows many who won't. Another student, Republican Benta Kleven, 26, says she is backing Obama. "He's going to change things," she says. ●

Cathy McDowell in Berlin: "There is no rural policy for the kind of rural we are."

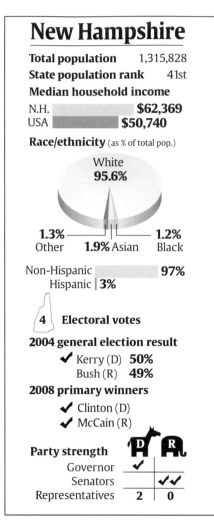

New Hampshire

Total population   1,315,828
State population rank   41st
Median household income

N.H.	**$62,369**
USA	**$50,740**

Race/ethnicity (as % of total pop.)

White
95.6%

1.3% Other   **1.9%** Asian   **1.2%** Black

Non-Hispanic   **97%**
Hispanic **3%**

4 Electoral votes

2004 general election result
✔ Kerry (D) **50%**
Bush (R) **49%**

2008 primary winners
✔ Clinton (D)
✔ McCain (R)

Party strength

	D	R
Governor	✔	
Senators		✔✔
Representatives	2	0

Rural America outgrows label

Communities fall through cracks of farm-driven policies

By Haya El Nasser • Excerpt from Wednesday, August 6, 2008 • BERLIN

As paper production increasingly moved overseas, the mill that helped boost the population of Berlin, New Hampshire to 30,000 went into bankruptcy. Now, a new owner is keeping it going with 400 workers, down from a high of 2,400.

"Once you peel the mill away, you have a city of 30,000 (housing) units but 10,000 people," says Cathy McDowell, executive director of the Family Resource Center in nearby Gorham. "There's blighted housing."

Locals tried to get federal funding to tear down some of the homes. They couldn't because there was a shortage of housing at the time in most of "urban" America.

In a nation whose urban needs influence federal policy and whose rural policy is dominated by agriculture, rural areas that have urban-style woes can fall through the cracks.

"One policy doesn't fit all," says Mil Duncan, director of the Carsey Institute at the University of New Hampshire.

The institute just issued a report based on surveys of 8,000 people in 19 rural counties. Its findings emphasize that 21st-century rural America is not just about farming.

Home to 17% of the nation's population, rural areas consist of at least four distinct regions that face contrasting problems. According to the report, the four rural Americas are:

• Amenity-rich where mountains, lakes, coastlines or forests draw vacationers, retirees and second-home owners.

• Declining resource-dependent that once thrived on agriculture, timber, mining and manufacturing—industries that have declined because of globalization and depleted resources.

• Chronically poor. These are regions such as the Mississippi Delta where residents and the land have seen decades of dwindling resources.

• In transition. Traditional resource-based economies are in decline, but these areas have natural beauty that offers potential for growth in service economies and niche industries.

In its most recent farm bill, Congress set aside $4 million a year for a new rural development program, says Chuck Hassebrook, executive director of the Center for Rural Affairs. "If policy is based on this assumption that rural is really about agriculture, then the vast majority of rural America is left out," he says. ●

Anne Soteros of suburban Philadelphia: "I'm right-to-life. It's always been important to me."

Pennsylvania

Total population	12,432,792
State population rank	6th

Median household income

Pa. **$48,576**
USA **$50,740**

Race/ethnicity (as % of total pop.)

White **85.6%**

1.2% Other
2.4% Asian
10.8% Black

Non-Hispanic **96%**
Hispanic **4%**

21 Electoral votes

2004 general election result

✓ Kerry (D) **51%**
Bush (R) **48%**

2008 primary winners

✓ Clinton (D)
✓ McCain (R)

Party strength	**D**	**R**
Governor	✓	
Senators	✓	✓
Representatives	11	8

Pennsylvania no slam-dunk for Democrats

Voters' anxieties about economy, Obama make a win unsure

By Kathy Kiely • Excerpt from Wednesday, October 15, 2008 • FOREST HILLS

At Rep. Mike Doyle's annual picnic here in this Pittsburgh suburb, Janet Keane recalled coming home during the Depression, when "honest to God, there was nothing to eat."

Keane, 85, said that she's looking for someone who will spare her grandchildren that experience as she tries to decide between Democrat Barack Obama and Republican John McCain in the presidential election Nov. 4.

At the Jenkintown Jazz Festival weeks earlier in the Philadelphia suburbs, social worker Ron Fisher worried about Obama's prospects. "America is trying to find any excuse not to elect him because he's a black man," he said.

The two conversations at opposite ends of the state sum up why McCain and Obama are continuing to compete fiercely for Pennsylvania's 21 electoral votes.

On paper, the state should be a slam-dunk for Obama: The last Republican presidential candidate to win the state was George H.W. Bush, the father of the current president, in 1988. Democrats also have doubled their edge this year in voter registrations from Republicans, up from a 600,000 lead over the GOP last year to 1.2 million as of last week, in part because the Illinois senator has been engaged in a massive effort to sign up new voters.

Republicans such as former governor Tom Ridge hope McCain's military record and conservative views on issues such as abortion will appeal to voters in a state

where military veterans are 14% of the population and Catholics are 30%.

"We have to win it," said Ridge, a co-chairman of McCain's campaign. "The candidate who wins Pennsylvania wins it all."

Democrats are countering with Biden, whose blue-collar upbringing in Scranton and familiarity to voters in the eastern part of the state—where the Delaware senator is a regular on Philadelphia TV news shows—make him an asset here.

Some of Obama's supporters believe that his difficulty in Pennsylvania has nothing to do with the issues. "The hardest part is trying to convince people because he's African American," said Anthony Mosesso, a Democratic committeeman on Pittsburgh's South Side. ●

Mary Alice Phillips, with daughter Annie, at the Oregon Trail Nature Park near Belvue, Kansas, says the choice of Sarah Palin created excitement and "reassured me about the Republican ticket."

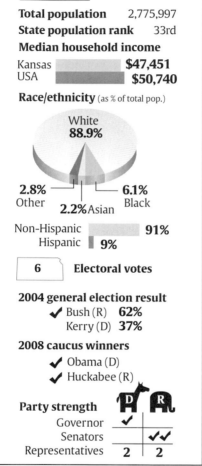

Kansas

Total population	2,775,997
State population rank	33rd

Median household income

Kansas	**$47,451**
USA	**$50,740**

Race/ethnicity (as % of total pop.)

White **88.9%**

2.8% Other
2.2% Asian
6.1% Black

Non-Hispanic **91%**
Hispanic **9%**

6	Electoral votes

2004 general election result
✔ Bush (R) **62%**
Kerry (D) **37%**

2008 caucus winners
✔ Obama (D)
✔ Huckabee (R)

Party strength

	D	R
Governor	✔	
Senators		✔✔
Representatives	2	2

Kansas politics bleeds two shades of red

Palin pick props up McCain

By Andrea Stone • Excerpt from Monday, October 20, 2008 • TOPEKA

Laura Ostrowski was "not particularly excited" about John McCain. Rocking her infant son, Matthias, in a sling at the Kansans for Life office here, Ostrowski says she didn't like McCain's support for research on human embryonic stem cells, which she sees as abortion. She saw the Republican as the lesser of two evils.

Then Sarah Palin came along.

"She's somebody a lot of women can identify with. She's a mom. She works. She's conservative," Ostrowski, 23, says of the Alaska governor. "It made me feel I was voting for him rather than against Obama."

Kansas politics may match the color of Dorothy's ruby slippers in The Wizard of Oz, but Republicans in her home state come in two shades of red that often clash. At one end of the spectrum are social conservatives who protest at abortion clinics and push to teach creationism in school. At the other are pro-business moderates who have crossed over to vote for centrist Democrats such as Gov. Kathleen Sebelius.

"McCain has really bridged that divide," says Thomas Frank, author of What's the Matter With Kansas? How Conservatives Won the Heart of America. "The country club set really like McCain, and values voters really like Palin."

Until the Arizona senator chose Palin as his running mate, the Republican rift briefly raised the possibility that Barack Obama could become the first Democrat to carry Kansas since Lyndon Johnson in 1964. Enthusiasm ran highest in January, when Obama, whose mother grew up in Kansas, visited his grandfather's hometown of El Dorado.

The connection helped Obama defeat Sen. Hillary Rodham Clinton in the caucuses. It also energized Democrats, who have registered twice as many new voters as Republicans have this year. Voter registration ends today. As of Sept. 1, the GOP had 751,125 voters on its rolls, well ahead of the Democrats' 451,577.

"For the general election," Kansas State University political scientist Joseph Aistrup says, "the question is not whether McCain wins, but by how much." ●

Needs other means: Nicholas Alfonso, a longtime shrimper, is supplementing his income by crabbing.

Louisiana

Total population 4,293,204
State population rank 25th
Median household income

La.	**$40,926**
USA	**$50,740**

Race/ethnicity (as % of total pop.)

White **65.1%**

1.6% Other
1.4% Asian
31.9% Black

Non-Hispanic **97%**
Hispanic **3%**

9 **Electoral votes**

2004 general election result
✔ Bush (R) **57%**
Kerry (D) **42%**

2008 primary winners
✔ Obama (D)
✔ Huckabee (R)

Party strength

	D	R
Governor		✔
Senators	✔	✔
Representatives	3	4

Shrimpers struggle for survival on Gulf Coast

Cheap imports, storm-damaged infrastructure hurting industry

By Rick Jervis • Excerpt from Monday, August 11, 2008 • NEW ORLEANS

Pete Gerica learned to pull white shrimp from Lake Pontchartrain as a boy from his father, who learned from his father, who learned from generations of Spanish and Balkan settlers.

As white shrimp season opens today in Louisiana, wildlife ecologists and residents such as Gerica are wondering how much longer a generation of shrimpers can survive on the Gulf Coast. One of the region's most storied professions has been at the center of a perfect storm that just won't quit.

In 2005, Hurricanes Katrina and Rita tore up homes, boats, ice houses, docks, processing plants and other things needed by shrimpers, said Rex Caffey, director of Louisiana State University's Center for Nat-ural Resource Economics & Policy.

"The shrimping industry took it on the chin more than any other commercial sector on the Gulf Coast," Caffey said. Just as the industry began to rebuild after the storms, fuel prices shot up, creating another obstacle, said Deborah Long of the Southern Shrimp Alliance, a regional advocacy group based in Tarpon Springs, Fla.

"We're very close to the point where we need to decide whether we're going to keep going or not," said Gerica, 55, whose ancestors were Yugoslav fishermen. "If you have to keep scratching to make a living, it's not worth it."

Americans eat more shrimp than any other seafood, 1.3 billion pounds a year, ac-cording to the National Fisheries Institute. About 90% of that shrimp comes from abroad. Since 2000, shrimpers have been threatened by an influx of cheaper shrimp from such countries as Brazil and Thailand.

These imports forced a dramatic drop in the per-pound price of local shrimp, said Martin Bourgeois of the state Department of Wildlife and Fisheries.

In 1987, the average dockside price per pound of shrimp caught in state waters was $1.45, said Bourgeois. By 2006, that price had dropped to 94 cents per pound.

"We started seeing fishermen abandoning the fisheries. And we're still seeing it," Bourgeois said. ●

Bill and Hillary, on the trail again

Senator, seeking a boost in Iowa, brings along a heavyweight

By Richard Wolf • Excerpt from Tuesday, July 3, 2007 • DES MOINES

Bill Clinton, one of the great campaigners of his generation, tried to help his wife without overshadowing her.

Behind in the Democratic money race and trying to pull ahead in Iowa, Hillary Rodham Clinton deployed her presidential campaign's ace in the hole Monday: her husband.

Former president Bill Clinton joined the New York senator for three days of campaigning across the state, to be followed by events this month in New Hampshire. Monday's rally drew several thousand sign-waving people to the Iowa State Fairgrounds. With five more rallies today and Wednesday, they were sure to enliven the Democratic race as it enters the final six months before Iowans start the voting in their caucuses.

Bill Clinton's role here is to tout his wife's credentials but not to overshadow her, and he did just that Monday. He spoke for less than 10 minutes, calling her "by a long stretch the best-qualified non-incumbent I have ever had a chance to vote for in my entire life."

He added, "I'd be here tonight, if she asked me, if we weren't married."

Noting her husband's oratorical skills, Hillary Clinton took the microphone and said, "If I was as smart as Bill seems to think I am, I would say nothing." Then she spent 30 minutes disparaging the Bush administration and outlining her goals on health care, energy, education and foreign policy.

"I will work my heart out for you," she

AP Images

said. Then, pointing at the ex-president seated beside her, she added, "I will have some good help along the way."

Many in the crowd, sitting on bales of straw and sporting buttons that read "Miss Bill? Vote Hill," were drawn by the ex-president's star power. "It's too bad he couldn't run for a third term," said Phyllis Thomas, 69, a retired state employee trying to choose between Hillary Clinton and Barack Obama. If Hillary wasn't a Clinton, "I wouldn't give her a second thought," Thomas said.

Bill Clinton remains popular among Democrats here and across the country. Even when he left the White House in 2001 following a sex scandal and impeachment by the House, his favorable rating in Iowa was 55%.

Therein lies the rub for Hillary Clinton: How to get more of her husband's star appeal to rub off without having him upstage her or remind voters of his administration's controversies.

"I think he could hurt," said Pam Clark, 64, a retired factory worker who showed

up more than two hours early for Monday night's rally. "He lied about things in the White House. Maybe he's lying now."

"I think it probably cuts both ways," said Ann Selzer, who conducts the Iowa Poll for *The Des Moines Register*. "There's residual good will towards former president Clinton. That may help bolster Hillary." But she said the New York senator must show how she will handle attacks on her husband's administration, which Selzer said still carries a "taint."

The events here represent the first time Bill Clinton has campaigned for his wife other than at fundraisers. They come at a time when Hillary Clinton is clearly ahead in many national polls and in most states, but not in Iowa nor in the crucial race for campaign cash.

Enter Bill Clinton, a prodigious fundraiser who quickly sold out 3,500 tickets to the Iowa Democratic Party's annual Jefferson-Jackson Day dinner last October. "People look forward to seeing him. He is a great orator," said Scott Brennan, the state's Democratic chairman.

Sen. Hillary Rodham Clinton, speaks at a barbecue in Fort Madison, Iowa, Monday, April 2, 2007.

The former president already talks about his wife's career and qualifications on a video on her campaign's website, www.hillaryclinton.com. On the campaign trail, "He's going to be talking about her, and she's going to be talking about the country," said Phil Singer, the campaign's press secretary.

The Iowa caucuses are scheduled for Jan. 14, followed by contests in Nevada, New Hampshire, South Carolina and possibly Florida. Then in early February, states such as California, New York and Illinois could all but decide who gets the two parties' nominations.

The Iowa Democratic caucuses next year could go down to the wire, as they did in 2004. For Clinton, "That's not necessarily a bad thing at this stage," Selzer said. "What you want to do is catch fire at the end." ●

Can Edwards win with an "us vs. them" pitch?

Populist message poses a challenge second time around

By Judy Keen • Excerpt from Wednesday, March 14, 2007 • OTTUMWA, Iowa

Dan Murphy, a Democrat and a sixth-grade teacher, is shopping for a presidential candidate in a community college conference room on a sunny Saturday. He's here to hear John Edwards' pitch.

Murphy, 50, likes Sen. Barack Obama but says the Illinois freshman "hasn't been around long enough." New York Sen. Hillary Rodham Clinton is "too much of a Washington politician." Edwards, he says, "is pretty down to earth and knows what's going on with people at my income level."

Murphy's assessment of the candidate in broken-in jeans, blue shirt and yellow "Live Strong" wristband is exactly what Edwards hopes to achieve in his second presidential run.

This time, the 2004 vice presidential nominee has a repackaged message framing the campaign as a struggle that pits the political and corporate elite against regular people who just want to make a decent living, afford health care and end the Iraq war. Edwards, who made millions as a personal-injury lawyer taking on big business, tells audiences he understands that they feel squeezed because they "pay more for everything ... but their pay is not going up."

Edwards' challenge is to convince voters in primaries and caucuses that he is a populist who would put their interests above those of big corporations and big govern-

ment. He must prove that message will triumph over the personal and political appeal of Clinton and Obama, and sell across the nation, especially to moderate and independent voters important in a general election.

David Rohde, a political science professor at Duke University, says the time might be right for a resurgence of populism. "What would make it even more plausible is if the economy went into a tailspin. ... The appeal of populism is class-based, on behalf of the people at the bottom of the economic spectrum when economic power is divided very unevenly."

Edwards welcomes the label. "If the word populist means that I stand with ordinary Americans against powerful interests, the answer's yes, but that phrase is sometimes used in an old, backward-looking way," he says in an interview with USA TODAY. His brand of populism is "very forward-looking," based on big ideas that will help all Americans, he says.

Edwards' new house in North Carolina has become a symbol of what some see as a contradiction between his political image and the way he conducts his life. His challenge is to ensure that voters don't decide that it negates his populism.

Aerial photos of the 102-acre estate show a 28,000-square-foot home that's

worth about $4 million and includes a recreation building with basketball and squash courts and swimming pool.

Ricci Boldt, 66, an undecided voter at Edwards' meeting here, knows all about the mansion. "So what? He worked for it," she says.

Edwards refers to his former Capitol Hill colleagues as "all that crowd in Washington." He warns voters to be skeptical of his rivals. "Don't you love it when they promise what they're going to do?" he asks. At three Iowa community meetings Saturday, there are no shout-outs to the man at the top of 2004 Democratic ticket, Massachusetts Sen. John Kerry, but he thanks union workers at every stop.

In a 40-minute interview, he attributes the evolution of his ideas to the fact that he's "more seasoned now that time has passed and I've been working, and I think I have more depth and maturity because of all that." He headed the Center on Poverty, Work and Opportunity at the University of North Carolina between campaigns.

"I think on this thing about a shifting," he says. "The truth of the matter is the country is in a place where it needs more dramatic, more transformational change."

Edwards has visited Iowa almost 20 times since 2004, and a poll last month of

John Edwards with New Mexico Governor Bill Richardson, Sen. Hillary Clinton of New York, and Sen. Barack Obama of Illinois, in a televised debate at the Dana Center of the Saint Anselm College in Manchester, New Hampshire, on January 5, 2008.

likely Democratic caucus-goers here showed him leading with 24%, followed by Clinton and Obama with 18% each. Edwards was the choice of 36% of caucus-goers in December, before most candidates' announcements. Kerry won Iowa's caucuses in 2004; Edwards was second.

Edwards' events don't attract as many people as Obama's do. Edwards' meetings on health care attract crowds that four years ago would have been considered large with the caucuses still 10 months away: 250 people here and in Newton, 500 in Burlington. Obama drew 2,300 people Saturday in Dubuque and 4,000 in Davenport.

Many Iowans approach their political duties as a sort of part-time job. They're diligent about showing up to hear candidates' pitches. And on this balmy day, several people say they already have narrowed their options to Edwards or Obama. ●

America Speaks • 41

The big question about Barack Obama

Does he have enough experience to be president?

By **Judy Keen** • Excerpt from Wednesday, January 17, 2007 • CHICAGO

Two years in the U.S. Senate. Seven years in the Illinois Senate. One loss in a primary election for the U.S. House of Representatives. One stirring keynote address at a Democratic National Convention. Two best-selling books.

That's Barack Obama's political resume. Is it enough to qualify him to be president?

"Sure," says Carol Hood, Democratic Party chairman in Calhoun County, Iowa. "Anymore, that might be a good factor," she says. "He doesn't have a lot of people he owes things to."

"Probably not," says Matt Pearson, Democratic Party chairman in Buena Vista County, Iowa. "He could use a little more experience," he says. "A lot of the people I know say they really like him, but just don't think it's his time yet."

Obama wouldn't be the youngest presidential nominee or chief executive. William Jennings Bryan was 36 when he first became a Democratic nominee. John F. Kennedy was 43 when he was elected. Theodore Roosevelt was 42 when he was sworn in after the assassination of William McKinley.

Nor would Obama be the least experienced nominee or president. Wendell Wilkie had never been elected to any office before he became the Republican presidential nominee in 1940. Woodrow Wilson had

AP Images

been New Jersey's governor for two years when he was elected in 1912. George W. Bush served six years as Texas governor before being elected president.

"Obama's inexperience is the big question mark about his candidacy," says Rep. Beth Arsenault, a Democrat who was just elected to the New Hampshire Legislature.

"It's not a deal-stopper necessarily," she says, "but two years in the Senate? It's not a lot."

David Axelrod, Obama's political strategist, says presidential campaigns aren't ultimately about candidates' job histories.

"Campaigns themselves are a gantlet in which you get tested," he says. "People get to see how you handle pressure and how you react to complicated questions. It's an imperfect and sometimes maddening system, but at the end of the day it works, because you have to be tough and smart and skilled to survive that process."

Some legislators who worked with Obama in the Illinois Senate say he proved he can overcome gaps in experience with his ability to quickly grasp complicated issues.

Republican Sen. Kirk Dillard, who took office in 1993, says he gravitated to Obama when the rookie arrived in Springfield in 1997.

"Sen. Obama was someone who I thought—and I was right—could tackle extremely complex things like ethics reform, the death penalty or racial profiling by law enforcement," Dillard says.

Richard Norton Smith, a historian who has run several presidential libraries and museums, says it would be better for Obama's sake, not to mention for the country's, if he had more experience.

"As Obama's supporters often point out, Abraham Lincoln was a former member of the Illinois Legislature who had served briefly in Congress before becoming president. But the parallels in the men's careers are no indication of success for Obama," Smith says. "Sometimes the election of inexperienced candidates whose charisma is their greatest asset produced great presidents, and sometimes it produced decidedly mediocre ones," he says.

Nicole Schilling, chairman of the Democratic Party in Greene County, Iowa, says

Barack Obama and David Axelrod exit their plane in Reno, Nevada, in August 2008.

Obama's lack of a long political record will work to his advantage. "Some people are saying he's young, he needs to wait," she says. "I think it's going to work to his advantage here.... He's kind of a blank slate, and people are projecting what they think onto him."

Obama's experience is broader than his time in elected office. He was a community organizer in Chicago and led voter-registration drives. He taught constitutional law at the University of Chicago. He lived for a time in Indonesia, a Muslim country. He has traveled to the Middle East, Africa and Iraq.

"He has lived abroad and has relatives who are certainly not your Mayflower Americans and understands different cultures," Dillard says. "Many presidents with foreign-policy experience have not lived firsthand the type of life that Barack has." ●

Dodd:

"I'm a late bloomer as a father," Christopher Dodd tells [a gathering of] Iowa teachers, putting aside a wonkish text on education policy in favor of more personal remarks in the cavernous Hilton Coliseum at Iowa State University. At age 62, Dodd—renowned in Washington gossip columns as a rakish man-about-town before he married in 1999—has two daughters, 5 and 2.

Grace was born two days after the Sept. 11, 2001, terrorist attacks, Dodd recalls, at a hospital in suburban Virginia that had a view of the burning Pentagon. "I wondered what kind of country she would have," he says.

That "sense of urgency" and a belief that the Bush administration has "squandered" the wealth and reputation of the USA prompted him to run for president, he says.

He emphasizes his expertise on foreign policy and work on children's issues, including his sponsorship of the 1993 Family and Medical Leave Act.

Richardson:

New Mexico Gov. Bill Richardson has run a state, served in a president's Cabinet and

and federal land management, he says. And, like nearly a quarter of Nevadans, he is Hispanic—though he tells a local TV crew, "With a name like Richardson, it's hard to get people to believe that."

Biden:
After delivering the biggest laugh line at the first Democratic presidential debate, Sen. Joe Biden said what's funny to him is that people seemed so surprised that he can tell a joke.

His deadpan, one-word answer, "Yes," Thursday night to a question about whether he could reign in his verbosity not only brought him media attention but scored points with voters and key lawmakers in a state where the second-tier candidate hopes to make his mark in 2008.

"I'm beginning to realize what I should have known all along," he said during an interview at his Columbia hotel. "Part of this is reintroducing myself to the Democratic Party, reintroducing myself to (young members of the media). I found it unusual that someone would think, 'God, Biden was humorous.' "

gone around the globe solving diplomatic crises, but on a recent afternoon at a farmer's market street fair, the Democrat is having a hard time convincing people he's making a White House bid.

"I'm running for president," Richardson, 59, tells two women passing by, and their reaction is laughter. "Look at all the photographers!" he exclaims, waving at the small pack of press trailing him. "You don't believe me!"

In Nevada, Richardson hopes he has special appeal. "I am a Western governor, I know about Western issues" such as water

Gravel:
Different war, same opposition could best describe Mike Gravel's reason for seeking the presidency. The former Alaska senator and Vietnam War opponent has called for an immediate withdrawal of U.S. troops from Iraq. His low levels of fundraising and support in the polls didn't merit an invitation to the latest Democratic debate in Philadelphia.

Kucinich:
The Ohio congressman Dennis Kucinich appeals to the far left with impassioned anti-war and impeach-Bush appeals and socially liberal positions. But his out-in-left-field status was probably enshrined forever when he acknowledged in an Oct. 30 debate in Philadelphia that he had once told the colorful actress Shirley MacLaine that he had seen a UFO, and that he had felt "a connection" in his heart and "heard directions" in his mind.

Giuliani: Can hero of 9/11 win over his own party?

Views on social issues could cost him Party's nomination

By Susan Page • Excerpt from Thursday, February 1, 2007 • BRETTON WOODS, N.H.

R udy Giuliani would seem to have all the credentials a candidate for president could want: A hero of 9/11, a crime-busting federal prosecutor, a two-term Republican mayor in an overwhelmingly Democratic city and one of the most admired politicians in the country.

He's got a big problem, though. First, he has to be nominated by Republicans who don't yet know his views on social issues.

"People remember how he provided leadership at a time the city needed it and the country needed it," coin-company executive Jeff Marsh, 41, says as he waits to greet Giuliani at the annual dinner of the Littleton (N.H.) Chamber of Commerce. While Marsh's admiration of Giuliani the man is evident, his support for Giuliani the presidential candidate is no sure thing. Giuliani's advocacy of abortion rights gives him "some pause," Marsh says ruefully.

The question is this: Can the thrice-married New Yorker—a supporter of abortion rights, gay rights and gun control—win the nomination of a Republican Party that has become increasingly dependent on and influenced by conservative Christians?

Maybe not, says Tony Fabrizio, a GOP pollster who advised Bob Dole's 1996 presidential campaign.

"As a presidential candidate, Rudy Giuliani

should absolutely be taken seriously," Fab- rizio says. "As a contender for the Republi- can nomination, he should be taken significantly less seriously. He has the stature to be president, but how does he get the Republican nomination? That is the fundamental disconnect."

Republicans tend to stick with front-run- ners. In each of the last nine presidential elections, the GOP contender who led the field the year before the election has won the nomination. Despite Giuliani's edge at the starting line, however, there is wide- spread skepticism among insiders such as Fabrizio whether he'll be there at the finish.

With the war in Iraq raging and terrorism a global threat, Giuliani's campaign could measure just how powerful social issues con- tinue to be in the GOP. "He may be the candi- date to test that proposition," says former Republican national chairman Ed Gillespie, now the party's state chairman in Virginia.

Dubbed "America's mayor" after he led New York City's response to the Sept. 11 at- tacks, Giuliani had a nearly 4-1 favorable rating among all those polled. McCain had a

2-1 favorable rating, and the rating for Dem- ocratic hopeful Hillary Rodham Clinton was only a bit more positive than negative.

"I have great admiration for how he han- dled everything in New York," says Jan Mercieri, an independent married to Little- ton's fire chief. She's brought a book profil- ing first responders who died during 9/11 for Giuliani to autograph before he speaks to the dinner. It's being held at the Mount Washington Hotel here, where the Bretton Woods monetary conference convened after World War II. ("God bless you for your service to our people and God bless Amer- ica," he writes.)

"I think it touched everybody," she says of his take-charge actions on that day, tears welling in her eyes even now.

As fondly remembered as Giuliani is for responding to Sept. 11, however, most Amer- icans don't know much else about him. Barely one in five Republicans knew that he supports abortion rights and civil unions for same-sex couples, the USA TODAY poll found. Nearly as many thought he was "pro- life" as said he was "pro-choice."

When they were told about his stance on those issues, his star dimmed. One in five Republicans said his views would "rule him out as a candidate" they could sup- port. That included one-third of those who attend church every week, an important base of the GOP that makes up a third of party loyalists.

Another 25 percent of Republicans said his views made them less likely to support him, nearly double the proportion who said they made them more likely to support him.

Giuliani portrays himself as a strong leader who can be trusted despite differ- ences he may have with a voter on a par- ticular issue.

"The single most important part of leader- ship...is to figure out what you believe, fig- ure out what's important, have convictions, stand for something," he says in his speech here, stepping to the side of the podium to get closer to the audience and punching his hand in the air for emphasis. "I would prefer to support for president or head of a corpo- ration, mayor, head of an anything—some- body who stands for something, even if I don't agree with them completely."

He cites a bipartisan trio—Abraham Lin- coln, Franklin Roosevelt and Ronald Rea- gan—as great presidents who earned support even from those who might have disagreed with them on this or that. "I don't even agree with myself on every- thing," he jokes. ●

In unsettled GOP field, Huckabee finds footing

Conservative tops new poll in Iowa

By Susan Page • Excerpt from Monday, December 3, 2007 • TILTON, N.H.

He's the anti-Rudy. Former Arkansas governor Mike Huckabee, the Republican long shot who in a new *Des Moines Register* poll has surged to the lead for the Iowa caucuses, could hardly be more different from the candidate who has led the GOP field nationally all year.

Former New York mayor Rudy Giuliani entered politics as a big-city prosecutor; Huckabee as a rural preacher. Giuliani is out of synch with the GOP's social conservative core; Huckabee is its most consistent champion. Giuliani's calling card is his leadership against terrorism after the 9/11 attacks; Huckabee has less experience on defense and foreign policy issues than any of his chief rivals.

The two candidacies offer dramatically different paths for a Republican Party now struggling to define and sell itself to voters. Should the GOP be led by an often-caustic, opera-loving New Yorker who vows to battle radical Islam? Or a joke-cracking Southerner who raises income inequality as an issue and favors classic rock and contemporary Christian music on his two iPods?

The chasm between him and Giuliani on the issues they emphasize and the regional cultures they represent "shows that the Republican Party is a bigger tent than the Democrat Party," Huckabee says. Perhaps, but it

"There's a curiosity factor," says chamber President Tim Sink. "It's an up-and-coming campaign, and he offers an alternative to the front-runners. It's another choice."

That evening, 150 people jammed a basement meeting room at the Chen Yang Li Restaurant in Bow for spring rolls and a chance to hear Huckabee's pitch.

Kathy and Rick Unger drove from Concord after work. They're leaning toward Giuliani but say they've been impressed by Huckabee's positive tone and sense of humor in the televised debates.

"He seems like a nice, honest person, and we need that," says Kathy, 45, who works for a health care company. But he lacks the experience in foreign policy and defense she'd like to see in wartime. Two of their four sons are in the military; one is being deployed to the Persian Gulf next February.

"Is a former governor of Arkansas ready to be president?" adds Rick, 47, the manager of a propane retail company and an avid Republican—a question for Huckabee and a shot at Bill Clinton.

In the interview, Huckabee defends his experience and expresses delight about the upward course of his campaign. What's his biggest worry these days?

"That I'll say something totally off the wall that will be taken the wrong way," he replies. "I'm pretty free-wheeling ... but there's a danger in it, and I know that. And I know that I'm working without a net, literally. When you're on the high wire and there's no net under you, you can't afford many falls." ●

also underscores how unsettled the Republican contest is just a month before the Iowa caucuses—and reflects how no GOP contender has satisfied a majority of the party.

It's all provided an opening for Huckabee—an ordained Baptist minister who has always opposed abortion and raised his hand at one debate to say he didn't believe in evolution—to attempt the unprecedented. Democrats sometimes have chosen presidential candidates who emerged from obscurity; former Georgia governor Jimmy Carter in 1976, for example. But the GOP in modern times has never nominated a contender who started the race so far back in the pack.

On several fronts, Huckabee's message is different from his chief Republican rivals. He strikes a more populist tone, warning of the downsides of free trade and the dangers of relying on imported food, fuel and military equipment. He backs what proponents call the "Fair Tax," a consumption-based plan that would replace the income tax system with a federal sales tax.

Huckabee also talks more often and in greater depth about domestic issues. He calls for the health care system to do more to emphasize prevention, offering his own turnaround as Exhibit A: He lost 110 pounds and took up running after being diagnosed with adult-onset diabetes in 2003. On education, he talks at length about the importance of providing music and art education, both to reach some students and to enrich society.

In a stop at the Tilton School, a private boarding school founded here in 1845, he told middle and high school students gathered in the gym about the need to cultivate both the right and left sides of the brain, the sides associated with creativity and logic.

First, though, Huckabee—who has been playing electric bass since he was 11—strapped on a borrowed guitar to perform with student band Ramjam, playing the rock classic "Louie Louie" and then "Sweet Home Alabama."

When the Concord Chamber of Commerce scheduled a luncheon address by Huckabee, fewer than 30 people signed up to attend. In the 48 hours before the lunch, though, 100 more people called to reserve a seat.

McCain firm on Iraq war despite cost to candidacy

Maverick from 2000 ties fortunes to Bush

By Susan Page • Excerpt from Tuesday, February 27, 2007 • SPARTANBURG, S.C.

The Sugar 'n' Spice Drive-in is so jammed with supporters and prospective supporters that Arizona Sen. John McCain climbs onto a chair next to the soda fountain to be heard.

"Obviously, I have to talk to you about the war in Iraq," he says somberly as the crowd quiets. "All of us—all of us—are frustrated. All of us are angry because of the mishandling of the war. All of us are saddened by the loss of our most precious asset, and that's American blood."

Even so, the costs of retreat would be higher, fueling chaos in Iraq and drawing terrorists to U.S. shores, he says. "I want us to have patience. I want us to succeed."

There's no doubt about that. At stake in Iraq is not only President Bush's legacy but also the 70-year-old McCain's last hope for the White House. In a crowded field of candidates, he is the only full-throated defender of the increase in U.S. troop levels and the war itself.

In a turn that's nearly Shakespearean, McCain—Bush's chief rival for the Republican nomination in 2000 and a critic since then on everything from tax cuts to torture—finds his fate inextricably tied to the fortunes of his onetime adversary and the increasingly unpopular war he is prosecuting.

McCain's unyielding stance on Iraq has

bolstered him with Republican regulars but eroded his standing among the independents and crossover Democrats who boosted his presidential bid seven years ago.

McCain has "taken a very hard stand—that we need more troops—and that's not where the American people are," says James Thurber, director of the Center for Congressional and Presidential Studies at American University. "He's isolated over there in a position he can't really change easily, even if things go more poorly on the ground."

On other fronts, McCain has trimmed his sails in ways that suit his ambitions. The nation's most prominent political maverick is cultivating his party's conservative power centers, including some he derided the last time he ran.

He voted against Bush's tax cuts in 2001; now he promises to extend them. He called evangelical leaders Jerry Falwell and Pat Robertson "agents of intolerance" in 2000; now he is reaching out to Falwell and other prominent conservative Christians. He declares that Roe v. Wade, the Supreme Court decision that legalized abortion nationwide, should be overturned—a different

position than he took in a 1999 interview.

But on the issue that dominates the 2008 election—and with a determination that could be seen as steadfast or stubborn—McCain continues to argue that the invasion of Iraq was justified and the war there must be pursued.

"He's no fool; he knows this is not a popular position to take," says Robert Timberg, a McCain biographer and editor of *Proceedings: The Magazine of the U.S. Naval Institute.* "But when it comes to a matter of national defense, when it comes to being behind the troops—those are issues that ultimately have no meaning politically to him."

McCain's bloodlines aren't in politics, Timberg notes. He is the son and grandson of Navy admirals.

Orson Swindle, a Marine pilot shot down over North Vietnam in 1966, says the years he and McCain spent together in a POW camp forged a fierce resolve to avoid the mistakes that they believe damaged the United States then.

"John above all others has that sense of history," Swindle says. "He knows we cannot

John McCain in early 2008 at a campaign stop in Florida. McCain tied his fortunes to the success of the surge in Iraq.

afford to lose or be perceived as losing."

On stage in Vero Beach, McCain is confident and teasing, showing the dash of the decorated Navy pilot he once was. At the drive-in in Spartanburg, he sports a brown leather bomber jacket. To some, he has hero status: People in the audience hold cellphones over their heads to snap a picture and push forward copies of his best-selling *Faith of My Fathers* to be autographed.

"I admire what he stood up for as a POW" during the Vietnam War and his support for the president on Iraq, says Frank Horton, 68, a retired Navy man who has driven from nearby Boiling Springs to see McCain. Still, Horton worries that the boost in troops won't work. If so, he cautions, "we're going to have to rethink the whole thing." ●

Romney kicks off White House run

Ex-Mass. governor emphasizes Midwest roots

By Jill Lawrence • Excerpt from Wednesday, February 14, 2007 • DEARBORN, Mich.

Only one Republican presidential candidate has run a business, governed a state and turned an ailing Olympics into a success story. That record, Mitt Romney said Tuesday, makes him uniquely qualified to transcend Washington's "petty politics" and deliver change.

The former Massachusetts governor and venture-capital CEO, kicking off his campaign, said the country needs "innovation and transformation." He said "life-long politicians" won't make it happen.

"I do not believe Washington can be transformed ... by someone who's never run a corner store, let alone the largest enterprise in the world," Romney told supporters at the Henry Ford Museum in the state where he was born and raised.

Romney reprised his message later for about 300 people at the Iowa State Fairgrounds in Des Moines. South Carolina and New Hampshire, weather permitting, were on his itinerary today. All four states have early primaries or caucuses. The Michigan primary is tentatively set for Feb. 5.

The Michigan launch allowed Romney to focus on his Midwestern roots rather than the liberal state he governed until last month. But he said he has the same goals for the nation as he had for Massachusetts, including strong families, lower taxes and

affordable, portable health care.

In foreign policy, Romney said "America must regain our standing in the world" and define its international role "not only in terms of our might, but also by our willingness to lead, to serve and to share." He said he would forge closer partnerships with other nations to support moderate Muslims and block Iran's nuclear ambitions.

On Iraq, Romney stuck with President Bush—for now. "So long as there is a reasonable prospect of success, our wisest course is to seek stability in Iraq, with additional troops to secure the civilian population," he said.

Romney, 59, is trailing former New York mayor Rudy Giuliani and Arizona Sen. John McCain in national polls. But he has fundraising clout—he raised $6.5 million in one day last month—and other strengths that political experts say make him a contender.

"We elect governors for president, not senators and mayors of cities," says Ed Sarpolus, an independent pollster based in

Lansing. "Romney is very well positioned. He has a good organization. He is not divorced. And he's got a record."

Romney's challenges include his Mormon religion and changing positions on issues such as abortion, gay rights, emergency contraception and stem cell research. He has moved to the right on all of them.

He said Tuesday that "I believe in the sanctity of human life." He also said that "unelected judges" should not make laws. Gay marriage is legal in Massachusetts as a result of a state court ruling. Romney pushed for and won passage of a bill that puts gay marriage on the ballot.

Romney and his Democratic legislature enacted the country's first statewide, universal health-coverage plan. It treats health insurance like auto insurance—individuals must have policies. People with low incomes will pay less for coverage.

Walter Schmidt, 58, a Lutheran minister from Grosse Pointe Woods, called Romney "a good middle-of-the-road Republican.

Mitt Romney emphasized his public and private sector success in his bid for the Republican nomination.

Traditional, but not a far-right fundamentalist. That's what I think we need." He added, "I would prefer that he wasn't Mormon," but "the family values that he reflects are more important" than his faith.

Romney's wife, Ann, his five sons and their families were onstage with him here. He talked of his Michigan childhood and his late father George's careers as an auto executive and governor.

Romney attended Harvard law and business schools. He lost a 1994 Senate race to Sen. Edward Kennedy. In 1999, he became CEO of the struggling 2002 Winter Olympics in Salt Lake City. He averted financial ruin and ran an extensive security operation for the Games shortly after 9/11. ●

Paul:
For several sweltering days in August, Cheryl Scott and several other Nashville residents stood on downtown overpasses bearing 8-foot-long signs that urged rush-hour drivers to "Google Ron Paul."

"Ron Paul is no laughing matter. He's tapping into a side of the Republican Party that's never had its issues addressed," said David All, a GOP strategist and Internet expert. "And he's doing it by running a truly Web 2.0 campaign."

Paul's campaign spokesman Jesse Benton said his Internet popularity demonstrates that his message is resonating. Paul is the only GOP candidate who wants to immediately withdraw U.S. troops from Iraq. "These national polls are still about name recognition, and that's an obstacle we have to overcome," Benton said.

Hunter:
Rep. Duncan Hunter sees his opening in the race for the 2008 Republican presidential nomination as the conservative's conservative.

"I believe strongly in this nation that we can have a new American sunrise of opportunity, faith and freedom," he says. "I think this is a time for the type of leadership I can offer."

Hunter, 58, is a veteran congressman from eastern San Diego County who chaired the House Armed Services Committee for the last four of the dozen years that Republicans controlled the House of Representatives.

That job made him well-known to Capitol insiders and a favorite of defense contractors, who found in him a staunch supporter of the Pentagon and of high-tech weapons systems.

Thompson:
The complexities of Fred Thompson's bid for the Republican presidential nomination were on display to a mix of fans and undecided voters as he visited coffee shops Monday in the kickoff caucus state.

The former Tennessee senator's persona on the presidential campaign trail is not all that different from the heavyweight authority figures he has played as an actor. His style is low-key, his message is stern, he doesn't always give simple answers, and

he's not averse to delivering bad news.

Last week, he proposed a Social Security plan he concedes carries little if any political advantage: It would slow the growth of benefits and introduce individual accounts. On Monday, he said the U.S. military is stretched too thin, U.S. intelligence isn't what it should be, and the country can't have "guns and butter" forever if it wants to win the war on terrorism.

"If we do the same old things the same old way with the same old people, we're going to get beat bad," he said, and the audience in a jammed coffee shop erupted in applause.

Tancredo:

U.S. Rep. Tom Tancredo of Colorado, a leading voice against illegal immigration, announced his candidacy for the 2008 Republican presidential nomination.

Tancredo made his announcement on WHO host Jan Mickelson's radio program, "Mickelson in the Morning." Tancredo promised to make the fight against illegal immigration the cornerstone of his 2008 bid.

He joins a crowded field that includes better-known hopefuls such as former New York City mayor Rudy Giuliani and Arizona Sen. John McCain.

"The crisis of illegal immigration threatens not only our economy and our security but our very identity," Tancredo said in a statement released by his campaign. "That ends today."

Thompson:

Tommy Thompson formally entered the presidential race with an assertion that he fills two voids in the Republican field: He is "the reliable conservative" and he has creative ideas.

"All that people have to do is look at my record, and I am the one individual that they can count on," the former member of President Bush's Cabinet and four-term Wisconsin governor said on ABC's This Week.

"People feel Republicans lost their way in Washington," particularly by spending too much money, Thompson said. He added that Republicans are not coming up with "original new ideas."

Brownback

Sam Brownback called himself a leader on issues important to economic, social and compassionate conservatives. "I've stood with them. I've pursued and pushed these issues. I've been aggressive," he said in an interview Sunday. "That gives me an advantage over the others looking at the field."

Brownback has worked to fight AIDS,

poverty and genocide in Africa. He supports a constitutional amendment to ban gay marriage and overturning Roe v. Wade, the Supreme Court decision that legalized abortion nationwide. He proposes a personal tax code with a single rate and individual retirement accounts as voluntary alternatives to Social Security.

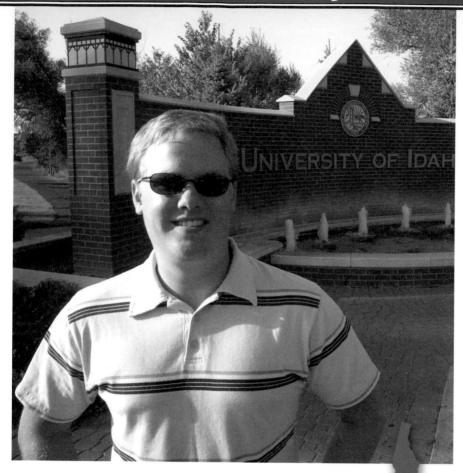

"This party is going places": Dylon Starry, a student at the University of Idaho, was a delegate to the Libertarian national convention.

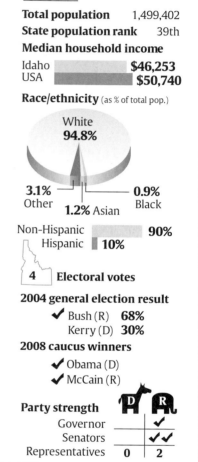

Idaho

Total population	1,499,402
State population rank	39th

Median household income

Idaho	**$46,253**
USA	**$50,740**

Race/ethnicity (as % of total pop.)

White **94.8%**

3.1% Other
1.2% Asian
0.9% Black

Non-Hispanic **90%**
Hispanic **10%**

4 Electoral votes

2004 general election result
- ✔ Bush (R) **68%**
- Kerry (D) **30%**

2008 caucus winners
- ✔ Obama (D)
- ✔ McCain (R)

Party strength

	D	R
Governor		✔
Senators		✔✔
Representatives	0	2

Big government gets Idaho grumbling

Libertarians hope to make gains in Republican state

By Karl Puckett • Excerpt from Friday, September 26, 2008 • MOSCOW

Dylon Starry, a senior at the University of Idaho, used to be a Republican, but on Nov. 4, he'll vote for Bob Barr, the Libertarian candidate for president.

Barr's message of less government and more individual rights fits the self-described "recovering Republican" like a new suit. The Democrats and Republicans spend too much of the public's money, he says. "That just brings us down, and Bob Barr would curb that significantly," Starry, 22, says in a chat at a coffee shop just off campus.

Across Idaho, the Iraq war and the Wall Street bailout fuel discontent with the major parties and a renewed willingness to consider Libertarian ideas, says Rob Oates, chairman of the Idaho Libertarian Party.

Oates, a Caldwell resident, sees an opportunity for Barr, a former Georgia congressman with a higher profile than any previous Libertarian candidate, to capture 3%, 4% or even 5% of the presidential vote in Idaho—significant but not decisive.

"I'm a hard-core Republican," says retired steamfitter-welder Vernon West, 66, standing on the front porch of his home in northeastern Idaho's Mullan. "There's no way in good conscience I could vote for Bob Barr."

A sign in the former Marine's front yard reads, "I'm a bitter gun owner. I vote," a reference to Obama's remark about some Americans who are bitter about the economy and cling to religion and guns.

McCain improved his standing with the state's Republicans when he picked a more conservative running mate in Alaska Gov. Sarah Palin, says Gary Moncrief, a political science professor at Boise State University. Palin was born in Sandpoint, Idaho, and graduated from the University of Idaho.

However, some in overwhelmingly Republican Idaho are not satisfied with the Republicans. "I have been a Republican my entire life, and we just felt like the Republican Party doesn't stand for less-intrusive government," says Harry McKinster, 45, a stock trader from Nampa, 20 miles west of Boise. He's voting for Barr. ●

Members of the Greenville Young Democrats, Kim Kegler and Drew Harkins, canvas homes along Timrod Way, in Greenville, South Carolina, as part of the Greenville "Walk for a Change."

South Carolina

Total population   1,107,709

State population rank   24th

Median household income

S.C.   **$43,329**
USA   **$50,740**

Race/ethnicity (as % of total pop.)

White **68.6%**

1.5% Other
1.2% Asian
28.7% Black

Non-Hispanic **96%**
Hispanic **4%**

8 Electoral votes

2004 general election result
✔ Bush (R) **58%**
Kerry (D) **41%**

2008 primary winners
✔ Obama (D)
✔ McCain (R)

Party strength

	D	R
Governor		✔
Senators		✔✔
Representatives	2	4

New voters in S.C. could help Obama

But McCain's VP selection has energized Republicans

By Ron Barnett • Excerpt from Wednesday, October 1, 2008 • GREENVILLE

Former Democratic National Committee chairman Don Fowler isn't ready to bet money on Barack Obama winning the Palmetto State in the Nov. 4 presidential election.

But Fowler said a confluence of factors makes it possible that this stronghold of Deep South conservatism could fall from the ranks of the GOP for the first time since it went to Jimmy Carter in 1976 and for only the second since John F. Kennedy took the state in 1960.

Fowler's arguments include:

• More Democrats turned out for their presidential primary in January than Republicans did for theirs, 529,000 to 443,000, according to South Carolina State Election Commission figures.

• The Obama campaign, energized by an overwhelming victory in the state primary, has been very active in registering new voters here.

• Obama campaigned heavily in South Carolina, which held the first primary in the South. He drew big crowds, particularly of young people.

Former governor Jim Edwards, who was elected in 1974 and was the first Republican governor of South Carolina since Reconstruction, said he thinks McCain "knocked a home run" when he chose Palin as his running mate.

State GOP Chairman Katon Dawson said his party isn't taking the state for granted, but he said he believes South Carolina voters will never go for "the most liberal De-

mocrat ticket we've faced in a long time."

According to the latest Rasmussen Reports poll released Sept. 20, McCain was apparently leading Obama 51% to 45%.

For some McCain supporters in Greenville, it's not so much a matter of being for him as it is being against Obama—and sticking to the party line.

Obama supporters see current economic conditions as ample reason to support Obama.

An Obama victory is still a long shot at best, according to Larry Sabato, director of the Center for Politics at the University of Virginia.

"If Obama even comes close in South Carolina, we'll have an early election night and a substantial Democratic victory for the presidency," he said. ●

Rhode Island's largest wind turbine hovers over subdivisions from its location at Portsmouth's Abbey School.

Rhode Island

Total population	1,057,832
State population rank	43rd

Median household income

R.I.	**$53,568**
USA	**$50,740**

Race/ethnicity (as % of total pop.)

White **88.7%**

2.3% Other — 2.8% Asian — 6.3% Black

Non-Hispanic	**89%**
Hispanic	**11%**

4 **Electoral votes**

2004 general election result

✔ Kerry (D) **59%**
Bush (R) **39%**

2008 primary winners

✔ Clinton (D)
✔ McCain (R)

Party strength

	D	R
Governor		✔
Senators	✔✔	
Representatives	2	0

Energy is major concern in Rhode Island

People want renewable, clean sources

By Charisse Jones • Excerpt from Monday, October 13, 2008 • PROVIDENCE

In this tiny coastal state, where government officials see wind and water as vital new pistons in their economic engine, energy tops many minds.

"People care quite deeply," says Karina Lutz, deputy director of People's Power & Light, a non-profit group focused on sustaining the environment and making energy affordable. "They want renewable energy. They want to save money on energy. And they don't want to see oil tar on their beaches."

Rhode Islanders are looking for the next president to reduce American dependence on foreign oil, to make the cars they drive more fuel-efficient and to harness the sun and other elements for heat and light. "The most important thing is looking at what we can do to sustain ourselves," says Kim Greenberg, 52, a dancer who lives in nearby Warwick.

Republican John McCain and Democrat Barack Obama both support development of renewable energy sources such as wind, solar and geothermal. Obama has said he would spend $150 billion over a decade to develop those sources, creating 5 million jobs. McCain has proposed a tax credit for businesses that research alternative energy sources, equal to 10% of their workers' salaries.

Some state officials say the next administration must accelerate the movement toward new kinds of power. "Both candidates talk a lot about energy policy," says Saul Kaplan, executive director of the Rhode Island Economic Development Corp. "We're hopeful that regardless of who wins ... we'll see serious progress over the next four years."

"We don't have oil, we don't have gas, we don't have uranium, but we've got water, and we've got wind," says Andrew Dzykewicz, commissioner of the state's Office of Energy Resources.

Rhode Island has nurtured health and life sciences, information technology and other industries. Officials hope energy will create another job sector.

Joe Caporelli, 42, likes both candidates talking about creating "green" industries and jobs.

"They want a new energy-based economy, which makes a lot of sense," says Caporelli, a cabinetmaker who lives in Smithfield. ●

Sen. Tim Johnson speaks to a group of constituents in the Hart Senate Office Building.

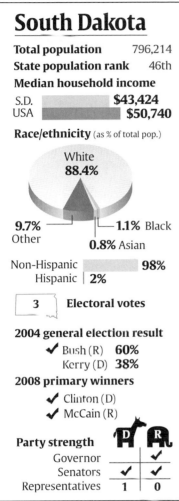

South Dakota

Total population	796,214
State population rank	46th

Median household income

S.D.	**$43,424**
USA	**$50,740**

Race/ethnicity (as % of total pop.)

White **88.4%**

9.7% Other

1.1% Black

0.8% Asian

Non-Hispanic **98%**
Hispanic **2%**

3 Electoral votes

2004 general election result
- ✔ Bush (R) **60%**
- Kerry (D) **38%**

2008 primary winners
- ✔ Clinton (D)
- ✔ McCain (R)

Party strength

	D	R
Governor		✔
Senators	✔	✔
Representatives	1	0

S.D. Democrats pin hopes on resilient senator

His popularity unlikely to rub off on Obama ticket

By Jeff Martin • Excerpt from Wednesday, October 15, 2008 • SIOUX FALLS

Sen. Tim Johnson has come through emergency brain surgery, a coma and a grueling recovery.

Now, Johnson, a 61-year-old Democrat who battled back from a December 2006 brain hemorrhage, is running for re-election in a GOP-dominated state where President Bush won 60% of the vote in 2000 and 2004.

It may turn out to be the easiest thing he's done in two years.

Johnson, running against Republican state lawmaker Joel Dykstra, was comfortably ahead 60% to 35% in a July Rasmussen Reports poll.

Johnson's popularity isn't likely to provide much help for Democratic presidential candidate Barack Obama against Republican John McCain in November.

The Obama campaign, though far behind, opened an office in downtown Sioux Falls in September. The office was set up for Obama, but "we think the interest in Obama and excitement for this campaign will help other Democrats down the ticket," said Matt McGovern, state director for the Obama campaign and grandson of 1972 Democratic presidential nominee McGovern.

Even though South Dakotans have a long history of helping Republicans win the White House, Johnson has prevailed since 1996, when he defeated three-term Republican Sen. Larry Pressler.

In 2002, he defeated Republican challenger John Thune. Two years later, Thune reached the Senate by beating Democratic incumbent Tom Daschle.

"Personalities matter a lot in a place like South Dakota," and Johnson was a likable candidate, says Kenneth Blanchard, a political science professor at Northern State University in Aberdeen.

The possibility Johnson might have had to step down were big issues for Democrats in 2006. The party's newly regained control of Congress was at stake.

Since returning to the Senate on Sept. 5, 2007, Johnson has used a motorized scooter to get from his office to the Capitol. His speech is still slurred, and he sometimes needs a few seconds to find answers to questions.

"I hoped all along I would stay in politics and do my state some good," Johnson says. "But I didn't know if I could. But as time went on, I grew ever more confident that I could run for office again." ●

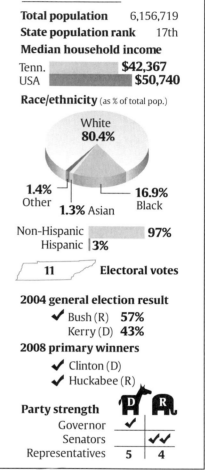

Conservative religious beliefs typically align with conservative political beliefs among Tennessee evangelicals.

Tennessee

Total population 6,156,719

State population rank 17th

Median household income

Tenn.	**$42,367**
USA	**$50,740**

Race/ethnicity (as % of total pop.)

White **80.4%**

1.4% Other

1.3% Asian

16.9% Black

Non-Hispanic	**97%**
Hispanic	**3%**

11   **Electoral votes**

2004 general election result
- ✔ Bush (R) **57%**
- Kerry (D) **43%**

2008 primary winners
- ✔ Clinton (D)
- ✔ Huckabee (R)

Party strength

	D	R
Governor	✔	
Senators		✔✔
Representatives	5	4

In Tennessee, evangelicals may hold the key

Democrats seek ways to make impact on socially conservative voters

By Clay Carey • Excerpt from Wednesday, October 8, 2008 • NASHVILLE

Dennis Barbee cares about low taxes. He also wants a strong economy and solid national security.

Above all else, the registered nurse from Spring Hill, Tenn., is basing his vote this November on moral issues.

"Making sure human beings have a right to live is important to me," Barbee says. He isn't sure whom he'll vote for, but the candidate he backs will be "a godly person that definitely has Jesus Christ as their savior," he says.

For conservative evangelical voters such as Barbee, presidential elections often hinge on social issues such as abortion or same-sex marriage.

Candidates push hard for the evangeli-cals' votes in Tennessee, the South and other states, such as Ohio and Kansas, says Heather Larsen-Price, a University of Memphis political scientist.

Democrat Barack Obama has spoken often about family values and social justice issues such as poverty, issues that resonate with a new generation of Christian voters, says James Hudnut-Beumler, dean of the Vanderbilt University's Divinity School.

Jessica Kelley disagrees with Obama's stance on abortion, but the wife of a United Methodist pastor says she is more concerned about poverty, health care and the war.

"I consider those moral issues ... a truly pro-life culture seeks not only to reduce abortions, but also to save lives at risk from hunger and lack of adequate health care and from the violence of war," says Kelley, who voted for George W. Bush in 2000 but plans to vote for Obama.

McCain's vice presidential pick, Alaska Gov. Sarah Palin, who is staunchly opposed to abortion, pumped new political energy into many white evangelical Protestants who had been lukewarm about the Republican candidate.

What makes conservative evangelical voters formidable, Vanderbilt's Hudnut-Beumler says, is the fact that they are usually on the same page politically. If a candidate can connect with them and they deliver at the polls, he says, evangelicals can "make an election." ●

Senator Robert Byrd has steered more than $3 billion to his home state in congressional earmarks.

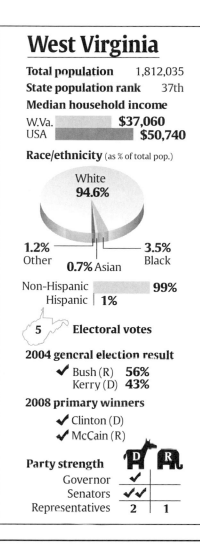

West Virginia

Total population   1,812,035

State population rank   37th

Median household income

W.Va.	**$37,060**
USA	**$50,740**

Race/ethnicity (as % of total pop.)

White
94.6%

1.2% Other **0.7%** Asian **3.5%** Black

Non-Hispanic **99%**
Hispanic **1%**

5 Electoral votes

2004 general election result

✔ Bush (R) **56%**
Kerry (D) **43%**

2008 primary winners

✔ Clinton (D)
✔ McCain (R)

Party strength	**D**	**R**
Governor	✔	
Senators	✔	✔
Representatives	2	1

Next president could dam up money flow to W. Va.

Sen. Byrd, state's benefactor, touts "common-sense investments"

By Richard Wolf • Excerpt from Thursday, September 18, 2008 • WHEELING

From the roof of the Robert C. Byrd Inter-modal Transportation Center on Main Street, one can see the Wheeling Artisan Center to the east, the Wheeling Stamping Building to the south and Wheeling Heritage Port to the west—all flourishing, thanks to the financial help of Sen. Robert Byrd.

To say the 90-year-old senator from West Virginia has brought home the bacon during his half-century in Washington would be akin to saying Congress likes to spend taxpayers' money.

Two of Byrd's Senate colleagues, Republican John McCain and Democrat Barack Obama, are threatening his ability to spend that money in places such as Wheeling, Charleston, Huntington and Morgantown. McCain wants to eliminate all congressional "earmarks"—money set aside by lawmakers for specific programs or projects back home. Obama favors less spending and more transparency.

Whoever becomes the nation's 44th president could send places such as Wheeling reeling.

"Without the government's assistance, I don't think we would have been able to develop what we have today," says Hydie Friend, executive director of the Wheeling National Heritage Area Corporation, which seeks to celebrate the city's place in history as the original gateway to the West.

The arguments against earmarks are familiar: The government can't afford them. They're chosen on the basis of politics, not merit. Lawmakers with clout command the most cash.

"What we've created here is an easy, corner-cutting way of getting money," says Leslie Paige of Citizens Against Government Waste, a non-partisan group opposed to earmarks.

That's not how West Virginia officials see it. Working in a largely blue collar state, where municipal governments and universities struggle to make ends meet, they see earmarks as a reward for entrepreneurial spirit.

Luckily, they have Byrd, who once said he wanted to be the state's "billion-dollar industry." Since 1991, he has helped send $3 billion home for highways and bridges, railroads and bus stations, research institutes and technology centers. This year, West Virginia ranked fourth in the nation for earmarks, with $179.80 per person. ●

Mill workers converse outside a loading area at NewPage prior to the start of a candlelight vigil organized by members of the United Steelworkers local and their families.

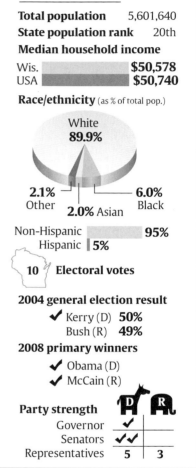

Wisconsin

Total population 5,601,640

State population rank 20th

Median household income

| Wis. | **$50,578** |
| USA | **$50,740** |

Race/ethnicity (as % of total pop.)

White
89.9%

2.1% Other
2.0% Asian
6.0% Black

Non-Hispanic **95%**
Hispanic **5%**

10 Electoral votes

2004 general election result

✔ Kerry (D) **50%**
Bush (R) **49%**

2008 primary winners

✔ Obama (D)
✔ McCain (R)

Party strength

	D	**R**
Governor	✔	
Senators	✔✔	
Representatives	5	3

Wis. paper industry troubles a priority

Jobs, economy major issues in tossup state

By Ben Jones • Excerpt from Thursday, October 9, 2008 • KIMBERLY

There's a campaign going on in this village of 6,444 in the northeast region of this battleground state.

Lawn signs line the sidewalks and organizers talk on cellphones in a temporary office.

The signs are not part of a political campaign. They carry slogans such as "World class work force" and "Save U.S. Jobs" and are part of an effort to save a paper mill, and maybe a town.

"What's happening here is the disappearance of a way of life for middle-class America," said Jim Dercks, a 29-year millworker.

Dercks was one of about 600 people who lost their jobs last month when NewPage of Miamisburg, Ohio, closed a paper mill it owned in Kimberly.

Wisconsin's paper industry produces everything from cardboard to newsprint and it has long been one of the state's signature industries. The industry is struggling under growing pressure from the economy and from foreign competition, according to Jeffrey Landin, president of the Wisconsin Paper Council, a trade group.

In a state such as Wisconsin, where presidential races frequently hang on paper-thin margins, the paper industry's decline could be an issue on Election Day.

Three mills have closed this year in the state, and, since 1998, the number of people employed in the paper industry has declined from 51,597 to 34,817.

"It makes people talk about the future and what proposals and what plans will candidates have to address an industry such as paper to protect the jobs that are here," Landin says.

In Kimberly, former mill employee Mark Van Stappen says, "Whoever can do the best for us, to get us working and stay working is going to be how most manufacturing people vote."

Angel Witt of Kimberly, an Obama supporter, thinks economic troubles could work in the Democrat's favor.

Jody Behling of Kimberly, a former plant employee said the candidate with the best solution to economic issues will probably win in Wisconsin. He said the "jury is still out" with many voters, but he supports McCain "because of his experience." ●

Savannah Conrad and Josh Franklin work at a diner in Casper that Obama visited before the Wyoming caucuses.

Wyoming

Total population 522,830

State population rank 51st
(rank list includes D.C.)

Median household income

Wyo.	**$51,731**
USA	**$50,740**

Race/ethnicity (as % of total pop.)

White
94.1%

4.0% Other

1.2% Black

0.7% Asian

Non-Hispanic	**93%**
Hispanic	**7%**

3	Electoral votes

2004 general election result

✔ Bush (R) **69%**
Kerry (D) **29%**

2008 caucus winners

✔ Obama (D)
✔ Romney (R)

Party strength

	D	R
Governor	✔	
Senators		✔ ✔
Representatives	0	1

Energy-rich Wyoming friendly for GOP

Some in deep-red state are less than fired up this year

By William M. Welch • Excerpt from Thursday, October 16, 2008 • MIDWEST

When delegates to the Republican National Convention broke into chants of "drill, baby, drill," they could have found no more receptive audience than here in Wyoming's oil patch, where workers have been doing just that for 100 years.

Like most of his colleagues, oil service worker Tyson DeVeny, 26, says he will vote for Republican John McCain for president over Democrat Barack Obama, in large part because the Republican ticket is viewed as friendlier to the oil business.

"This is our life: oil and gas and guns," says Curt Chapman, 36, a third-generation oil worker who says he doesn't know any-one who will vote for Obama.

Yet 45 miles away in Casper, Wyoming's largest city and one of its most Republican areas, there are some who are disappointed with the Bush administration and unenthusiastic about McCain.

"McCain will win, but it will be a lot closer than people think," says Phil Roberts, history professor at the University of Wyoming in Laramie.

What's more, Wyoming's economy is doing well. Wyoming has oil, natural gas and coal as its financial engine, and the state's cycles often run in opposition to the rest of the country, Roberts says. Wyoming is buoyed by high energy prices that keep unemployment low and produce healthy revenue for a state with no income tax and a low sales tax. Perhaps that is why McCain's campaign has little visible presence in the state.

However, Wyoming was good to Obama during his primary season contest with Hillary Rodham Clinton. He handily won Wyoming's Democratic caucuses in March.

"I thought he was wonderful," says Savannah Conrad, 24, a waitress at Johnny J's, a Casper diner Obama visited. A mother with a second child on the way, Conrad says she and her husband are enthusiastic about Obama and are most interested in affordable health care. ●

Governor Sarah Palin accepts the nomination for vice president at the Republican National Convention.

Palin pick bolsters Alaska lawmakers

Governor on Republican ticket may help endangered senator, congressman

By Ken Dilanian • Excerpt from Friday, October 17, 2008 • GIRDWOOD

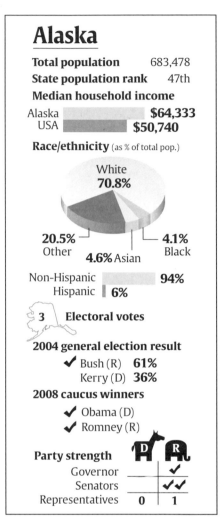

Alaska

Total population	683,478
State population rank	47th

Median household income

Alaska **$64,333**
USA **$50,740**

Race/ethnicity (as % of total pop.)

White **70.8%**
20.5% Other
4.6% Asian
4.1% Black

Non-Hispanic **94%**
Hispanic **6%**

3 Electoral votes

2004 general election result
✔ Bush (R) **61%**
Kerry (D) **36%**

2008 caucus winners
✔ Obama (D)
✔ Romney (R)

Party strength	D	R
Governor		✔
Senators		✔✔
Representatives	0	1

---

aura Bowen, an attorney and political independent, was determined to vote against Republican Sen. Ted Stevens, whose chalet in this picturesque ski town is at the center of his corruption trial in Washington as he runs for re-election. She was even flirting with supporting a Democrat for president.

Then came what she calls "the Palin hit job." Bowen says, "The Democrat smears against Palin and the biased media coverage have made it easy for me to vote a straight Republican ticket."

Palin's base is expected to turn out in big numbers, independent Anchorage pollster Ivan Moore says. As a result, her presence at the top of the ticket all but assures Alaska's continued spot in the Republican column for president, and it could improve the re-election chances of the state's two endangered Republican members of Congress, Stevens and Rep. Don Young, Alaska's only House member.

Palin on the ticket could be seen as a lifeline for the Republican incumbents, but it's not as simple as it seems. Palin hails from the Christian right wing of the party, Moore said, while Stevens and Young represent the pro-business wing.

Many Girdwood residents, even those who say they sometimes support Democrats, are willing to give Stevens the benefit of the doubt. He has done a lot for the state, they say, and the house at the center of the trial is no palace. "He probably made some errors, but I don't think he's a dishonest person," says Randy Brandon, who runs a photography business.

Rebecca Braun, editor of *Alaska Budget Report,* a non-partisan state political journal, says she senses that "a little bit of an upsurge of sympathy for Ted Stevens could sort of swell over and help Don Young, since they're often mentioned in the same breath, and there's this feeling that its a bit of a witch hunt against 'our guys in D.C.'" ●

Just Joe: Many voters in Delaware have a personal connection to Senator Biden.

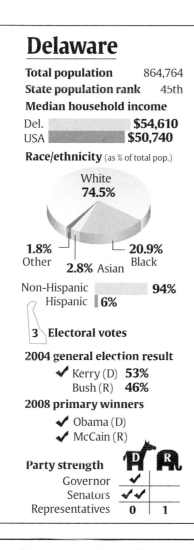

Delaware

Total population 864,764

State population rank 45th

Median household income

Del. **$54,610**
USA **$50,740**

Race/ethnicity (as % of total pop.)

White **74.5%**

1.8% Other
2.8% Asian
20.9% Black

Non-Hispanic **94%**
Hispanic **6%**

3 Electoral votes

2004 general election result

✔ Kerry (D) **53%**
Bush (R) **46%**

2008 primary winners

✔ Obama (D)
✔ McCain (R)

Party strength	D	R
Governor	✔	
Senators	✔✔	
Representatives	0	1

Though small in size, Delaware big on Biden

Even Republicans excited native son on national ticket

By Maureen Milford • Excerpt from Friday, October 10, 2008 • WILMINGTON

In this tiny state, where residents can run into their congressman at Home Depot, nearly everyone has a story about Sen. Joe Biden.

Such personal connections between voters and Biden could explain why many in Delaware, which is less than 2,500 square miles and has fewer than 900,000 people, are proud that he was tapped as the running mate of Democratic presidential hopeful Sen. Barack Obama.

To be sure, Biden has his detractors here, although even Republicans admit it's exciting to have a Delawarean on the national ticket.

"I liken it to a college buddy getting married. You might be happy that he's getting married, but you might not be glad he's marrying your sister," says Tom Ross, chairman of the state Republican Party.

Others haven't forgotten that when Biden ran for president in 1987, he cribbed from a speech by Neil Kinnock, then the British Labor Party leader. Biden apologized. By the time he dropped out of the race, there were other revelations.

He acknowledged that he had exaggerated his academic credentials at a New Hampshire campaign stop. There was a furor over his admission that in his first semester in law school, he used five pages of a law review article without proper attribution. Biden got an "F" and had to repeat the course.

"That, to me, shows a moral fissure in the man's character," says William Prickett, a retired lawyer and a supporter of Republican nominee John McCain.

Still, a Fairleigh Dickinson University's PublicMind Poll in September found that 65% of Delawareans have a favorable opinion of Biden, and 73% think he is a good choice for vice president.

"Politics becomes a lot more personal in Delaware because of the familiarity with the folks that get elected," says Brian Murphy, former treasurer of the state Democratic Party. "When he's in Delaware, more people call him 'Joe' than they call him 'Senator.'" ●

Running for third term: Sen. Susan Collins concludes a tour of the Maine Medical Center Research Institute in Scarborough, Maine.

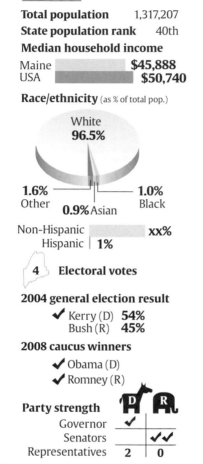

Maine

Total population   1,317,207

State population rank   40th

Median household income

Maine	**$45,888**
USA	**$50,740**

Race/ethnicity (as % of total pop.)

White **96.5%**

1.6% Other   **0.9%** Asian   **1.0%** Black

Non-Hispanic   **xx%**
Hispanic | **1%**

4   **Electoral votes**

2004 general election result

✔ Kerry (D)   **54%**
   Bush (R)   **45%**

2008 caucus winners

✔ Obama (D)
✔ Romney (R)

Party strength	**D**	**R**
Governor	✔	
Senators		✔✔
Representatives	2	0

In Maine, Collins an elusive target for Democrats

Despite unfavorable conditions for GOP, challenger gets little traction

By Martha T. Moore • Excerpt from Friday, September 19, 2008 • LEWISTON

Jimmy Simones greets a customer at his family's restaurant with this: "Crude prices are down. We're happy."

The price of oil, in a state where 80% of homes use it for heat, has supplanted politics as the lunchtime topic at Simones' Hot Dogs, a 100-year-old fixture here in the downtown of Maine's second-largest city.

It can take a Maine homeowner 1,000 gallons of heating oil to get through the winter and, at nearly $4 a gallon, residents here are dreading cold weather.

"There are some people that are going to freeze this winter because they have no money," says Betty Spugnardi, lunching at Simones' with her husband John.

Those high prices, a struggling economy and anger at President Bush have Democrats believing they could pick off Susan Collins, one of Maine's Republican senators. After all, Maine has voted Democratic in presidential elections going back to 1988. The governor and both House members are also Democrats.

She is a Republican in a state where independents and Democrats outnumber GOP voters, and a target of the national Democratic Party, which has sent money and staff to help Rep. Tom Allen, a 12-year Democratic House veteran.

So why isn't she in trouble? The same poll shows Collins sailing ahead by 19 points.

Allen can't seem to convince upstate voters that Collins is the closet conservative he

says she is. "People in Maine don't have a clue as to how she actually votes," Allen says.

Many Maine voters are conservative when it comes to taxes but less so about social issues. Allen has tried hard to undo Collins' moderate image, portraying her as a Bush supporter.

Collins points to Allen's 98% record of supporting Democratic Party positions. (He voted with Bush 4% of the time last year, according to Congressional Quarterly.) "The person who tows the party line is clearly Tom, not me," Collins says. "I am very much in the mainstream of New England moderate Republicans." ●

Troubled times: The paper mills have closed in Fitchburg, Massachusetts, on the Nashua River, and the city is in an economic slowdown.

Massachusetts

Total population   6,449,755

State population rank   14th

Median household income

Mass.	**$62,365**
USA	**$49,807**

Race/ethnicity (as % of total pop.)

White **86.5%**

1.7% Other

6.9% Black

4.9% Asian

Non-Hispanic **92%**
Hispanic **8%**

12 Electoral votes

2004 general election result

✔ Kerry (D)   **62%**
  Bush (R)   **37%**

2008 primary winners

✔ Clinton (D)
✔ Romney (R)

Party strength

	D	R
Governor	✔	
Senators	✔ ✔	
Representatives	10	0

Economic angst tops issues in Fitchburg

Residents of Massachusetts mill town fear losing their jobs and homes

By Susan Page • Excerpt from Monday, September 15, 2008 • FITCHBURG

Folks at the City Hall Cafe on Main Street are bracing for trouble. Waitress Mona Roberts starts a second job as a home health care worker this weekend. Proprietor John Karanasios is debating whether he could unscrew some of the light bulbs in the diner to reduce his $1,800-a-month utilities bill. Roger Nascimento, owner of a small house-painting business who has dropped in to grab a quick breakfast, may close off the second floor of his home and move his family downstairs this winter to save on heating costs.

"People are getting laid off because businesses are closing down, and I've got two friends who are losing their houses," Roberts says between refilling coffee cups and offering hugs to the regulars. Even tips are down as locals count their pennies.

Fitchburg was a thriving industrial center that featured a mile-long Main Street spotted with grand Victorian-style churches, three of them decorated with stained-glass windows from Tiffany's. Steep terrain rose on either side of the river, and residents boasted that they lived in the hilliest city outside San Francisco.

When the town's paper mills were in their heyday a century ago, locals say the river would run yellow one day, red the next—whatever color paper was being produced.

The river has returned to its natural color, which is a positive development environmentally but a troublesome one economically. Most of the big mills are empty. Crime, especially drug-related crime, is now a major concern.

"It's like a collision of things," says Robert Forrant, a professor at the University of Massachusetts-Lowell who studies the economies of small New England cities. "There's disappearing jobs, then the home foreclosure crisis and now high energy costs. All of that has made people feel a great deal of economic anxiety."

In the presidential election, both campaigns see Democrat Barack Obama as all but certain to carry the Bay State and its 12 electoral votes. Among the most reliably Democratic states in the nation, Massachusetts hasn't voted for a Republican presidential candidate since Ronald Reagan. ●

Barack Obama speaks to a crowd of supporters at a Chicago rally.

Obama and Huckabee start with a bang

Setbacks for Clinton and Romney, hope for Edwards as N.H. looms

By Susan Page and Jill Lawrence • Excerpt from Friday, January 4, 2008 • DES MOINES

Illinois Sen. Barack Obama scored a stunning victory over New York Sen. Hillary Rodham Clinton in the opening Iowa caucuses Thursday night, recasting the Democratic presidential race.

Among Republicans, former Arkansas governor Mike Huckabee reshaped that contest with a victory over a better-funded, better-organized rival, former Massachusetts governor Mitt Romney.

The Associated Press declared Obama and Huckabee the victors based on early returns from the caucuses held in firehouses, schools and community centers across the state.

The first contest of the 2008 presidential season Thursday set up titanic battles for both parties in the New Hampshire primary that follows in four days.

"Iowa is the Gettysburg of the nominating process," says Mark Mellman, a leading Democratic pollster who's not affiliated with a campaign. "Like Gettysburg, you have whole armies massed against each other, and there's no doubt the conflict is going to continue for weeks to come. But the outcome of this battle is going to determine the course of the war."

Among what he called "invisible" effects was a boost for Arizona Sen. John McCain, who has concentrated on New Hampshire.

Romney, his chief rival there, arrives in the state early this morning weakened from an opening loss.

"He has some explaining to do in New Hampshire without much time to explain," says Andrew Smith of the University of New Hampshire Survey Center.

The compressed primary calendar magnifies the impact of the first contests, Smith said. "The snowball effect is going to be incredibly difficult to stop."

The New Hampshire primary on Jan. 8 is followed by the Michigan primary on Jan. 15, Nevada caucuses on Jan. 19, South Carolina Republican primary on Jan. 19 and Democratic primary on Jan. 26.

Clinton, who consistently has led the Democratic field in national polls, had to wage a pitched battle here against Obama and former North Carolina senator John Edwards. Clinton and Edwards were locked in a tight battle for second place.

Iowans chose Obama's message of "turning the page" to a new kind of politics over Clinton's assurances that she had the strongest experience. She carried voters over 65 by 2-1, according to surveys of voters as they entered the caucuses, but Obama beat her by 5-1 among those under 30.

Former New Hampshire Democratic chairman Joe Keefe called Obama's victory "earth-shattering" and predicted he would benefit from the sort of boost that helped John Kerry in 2004 to victory in New Hampshire.

Among Republicans, Iowa became a showdown between Romney, who built a formidable organization, and Huckabee, whose operation relied on support from conservative Christians, gun clubs and home-schoolers. "Passion breeds organization," said Chip Saltsman, Huckabee's campaign manager.

The Republicans offered dramatically different faces between Huckabee, who served as a Baptist minister before entering politics, and Romney, who had a career in business. ●

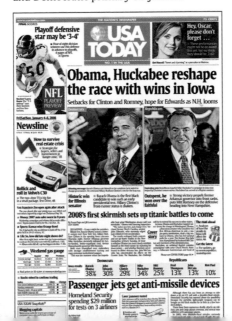

On the presidential campaign trail with Senator John McCain.

McCain rebounds in N.H.; Clinton defeats Obama

Results leave races for president wide open in both parties

By Susan Page • Excerpt from Wednesday, January 9, 2008 • NASHUA, N.H.

Republican presidential hopeful John McCain, counted out six months ago, scored a remarkable political comeback Tuesday, winning the New Hampshire primary over Mitt Romney. Among Democrats, Hillary Rodham Clinton edged out Barack Obama.

Political analyst Charles Cook called McCain's victory "the greatest comeback since Lazarus" and attributes it to "an enormous vacuum in the Republican Party."

With former Arkansas governor Mike Huckabee the winner in Iowa and McCain in New Hampshire—and former New York City mayor Rudy Giuliani still hopeful about winning Florida's primary on Jan. 29—"we may be settling in for a long haul on the Republican side," Cook said.

On an unseasonably balmy day, a record 500,000 people voted in the nation's first primary.

The results of the Democratic race buoyed supporters of Clinton, who had finished a disappointing third in Iowa. She had trailed by double digits in the USA TODAY/Gallup Poll and other statewide New Hampshire surveys in the last few days. Her husband, former president Bill Clinton, complained that the primary schedule and the news media had treated her unfairly.

Mallory Parkington, 32, of Concord took her 5-month-old daughter Kerris with her to vote for Clinton. Parkington had been on the fence between Clinton and Obama, but she said she was moved by news reports of Clinton near tears Monday as she described her feelings about the election.

Clinton "seemed a lot more real at that moment," she said. "It just made me decide to vote for her. They're pretty close on the issues."

McCain has been predicting a win in New Hampshire for days, too, and he was jubilant at a victory celebration for his supporters in Nashua. "Tonight we sure showed them what a comeback looks like," he said. "Thank you, New Hampshire, from the bottom of my heart."

McCain's candidacy was derided as over when he was nearly out of money and lost his top staff in a summertime overhaul. "Mac is back!" his supporters chanted, and "Johnny B. Goode" blared over the loudspeakers.

The loss was as stunning for Romney as the victory was for McCain. Romney had the best organization and aired the most TV ads. As the former governor of neighboring Massachusetts—and the owner of a lakeside home in New Hampshire—he had run almost as a favorite son.

Exit polls showed deep-seated distress among voters in both parties.

Voters expressed anxiety about the economy and concern about the Iraq war. Among Democratic voters, 30% said they were dissatisfied with the Bush administration and another 62% said they were angry. Even half of Republicans expressed negative views about the Bush White House. ●

Barack Obama and his wife, Michelle, are greeted by enthusiastic supporters at a Super Tuesday rally.

Democrats trade Super Tuesday victories, McCain continues surge

By Chuck Raasch • Excerpt from Thursday, February 7, 2008 • WASHINGTON

Super Tuesday turned into Split Tuesday, a big surge for John McCain, a moment of Southern redemption for Mike Huckabee and a nationwide confirmation of the difficulty Democrats are having choosing between Hillary Rodham Clinton and Barack Obama.

While Clinton and Obama traded wins and delegates through time zones, McCain appeared to be surging to a decisive delegate lead among Republicans. He won the big prize in California and bellwether Missouri.

But former Arkansas Gov. Huckabee's victories in four Southern states was the GOP surprise of the day, raising questions about Mitt Romney's claim for a conservative alternative to McCain and about McCain's appeal in the most reliably Republican region of the country.

Clinton took California, the Democrats' biggest prize, turning back a late Obama challenge, and relied heavily upon women to do it. But Obama won a majority of the Democratic contests. His victories included some of the nation's least diverse states in the Plains and Mountain West, a notable accomplishment for the candidate who would be the nation's first black president.

On a day in which the nation's midsec-tion was ripped with deadly storms, 24 states held primaries or caucuses, and they left neither party with a certain path to the nomination. But McCain is now the clear front-runner in the GOP.

By winning California and big states in the Northeast and Midwest, including plum winner-take-all states like Illinois and New York, McCain delivered clarity but not certainty to the GOP nomination fight.

"We must get used to the idea that we are the Republican Party front-runner," the Arizona senator said in Phoenix. "And I don't really mind it one bit."

Voters around the country spoke of many of the qualifications and reservations that have defined the candidates so far.

Obama "lacks experience but I like the principles he stands on," said Obama voter Richard Aguilar, 19, a freshman at the University of Illinois-Chicago. But Monica Geick, 19, another freshman at the university, said she changed her mind from Obama to Clinton in the past few days after watching the two debate on television.

"He seems like a good speaker and he seems like he's got that presidential aura," Geick said. "But when you listen to the debates, it seems like Hillary knows more what she's talking about."

Democrats may face a protracted fight—what Republican pollster Kellyanne Conway calls "a slow bleed to the nomination"—in part because Clinton and Obama are finding it difficult to draw distinctions between each other. Anything perceived as negative campaigning does not seem to be working with Democratic voters who have a hunger to win the White House and want a unified party. ●

John McCain and his campaign were revitalized after rolling to victory in the Super Tuesday primaries.

McCain wins, Clinton snaps Obama's streak

By Chuck Raasch • Excerpt from Wednesday, March 5, 2008 • WASHINGTON

Sen. Hillary Rodham Clinton rebounded behind firewalls in Ohio, and possibly Texas, in a dramatic "Survival Tuesday" that prolongs the Democrats' intense presidential nomination fight.

John McCain ended the Republicans' contest, sweeping four states and clinching a once-improbable GOP nomination. The 71-year-old Republican labeled his Democratic rivals as taxers and spenders, and said he was the true candidate of the future.

The final hours of the Republicans' nomination fight was much less dramatic, almost anti-climactic. Arizona Sen. McCain swept Ohio, Rhode Island, Texas and Vermont Tuesday and all his calendars now point to November.

"Now we begin the most important part of our campaign—to make a respectful, determined and convincing case to the American people," McCain told supporters in Dallas.

Arkansas Gov. Mike Huckabee, who had vowed to campaign until McCain hit the magic 1,191 delegates necessary to win the nomination, confronted that point of no return Tuesday night.

Huckabee called McCain and told him he would "do everything possible to unite our party, more importantly to unite our country so that we can be the best nation we can be."

Among Democrats, Clinton was benefiting from a gender gap among anxious voters in Texas and Ohio, where roughly six in 10

Democratic voters were women. Clinton also was winning decisively among Hispanic voters in Texas, according to network exit polls.

Obama carried white men in both states, and he carried voters under 30 by more than 2-1, the same margin by which Clinton won voters 60 and older. But in Ohio, senior citizens made up nearly a quarter of the Democratic vote, while those under 29 made up just 16 percent, according to the exit polls.

Obama confronted questions about his relationship to a fundraiser on trial for corruption in Chicago, and a dustup over what an Obama campaign adviser may have told Canadian officials about Obama's anti-NAFTA rhetoric. Media questioning of Obama got tougher, and even Saturday

Night Live parodied media treatment of the 46-year-old senator.

Even with her victories Tuesday, Clinton faces daunting delegate math.

The Associated Press had Obama with a 102-delegate lead—1,378-1,276—going into Tuesday. And during the day, Obama picked up three more superdelegates (party leaders or elected officials who can choose to support either candidate) in Texas, South Carolina and Georgia, respectively. It takes 2,025 to win the nomination.

Even if Clinton ended up with 55 percent of the 370 delegates at stake Tuesday—no sure thing given the intricate rules of the hybrid primary and caucus in Texas—she would still need to win 55 percent of the 601 delegates in the remaining dozen primaries and caucuses between now and June 7 to pull even with Obama. ●

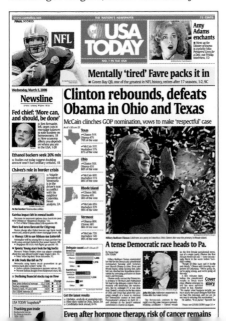

Hillary Clinton waves to supporters at the National Building Museum in Washington, D.C., where she ended her race for the Democratic presidential nomination and endorsed Senator Barack Obama on June 7, 2008.

Clinton backs Obama, suspends campaign

By Brian Tumulty • Excerpt from Thursday, June 12, 2008 • WASHINGTON

Four days after Barack Obama clinched the Democratic presidential nomination, Hillary Rodham Clinton officially suspended her own White House bid and endorsed the man she called "my rival" during an often contentious campaign

"I endorse him and throw my full support behind him," Clinton said. "And I ask all of you to join me in working as hard for Barack Obama as you have for me."

Clinton made the announcement at the National Building Museum, a tourist destination that drew hundreds of curiosity seekers along with campaign volunteers.

Clinton's formal concession speech was no surprise— an e-mail her campaign sent out shortly before 2 a.m. Thursday told supporters she would extend her congratulations to Senator Obama and her support for his candidacy.

But the speech was closely watched because some Clinton supporters, bitter over the sometimes bruising primary contest against Obama of Illinois, have threatened to stay away from the polls in November or vote for Sen. John McCain of Arizona, the presumptive Republican nominee.

McCain's campaign already is trying to woo that voting bloc. Sen. Joe Lieberman of Connecticut, a former Democrat turned independent, sent Democratic voters an e-mail Thursday urging them to join Citizens for McCain.

Some Clinton supporters said it would take more than one speech to get them to vote for Obama in November.

"My vote is not a given and I am going to use it carefully and wisely," said Donna Rasin-Waters, 50, a psychologist from Brooklyn, N.Y. "There are 18 million of us. I think we are not going to come over easily and lightly."

Jamie Schuman, 27, of Washington, said she had no qualms about making the switch to Obama.

Schuman, who stopped in at the Clinton speech after helping out at the 2008 National Race for the Cure to benefit breast cancer, said it's Obama choice "whether he wants to use her."

Another Democratic voter, Edwin Dun-

ston, 29 of Rockville, Md., said it could take a month for him to "get over it and actually look at Obama."

"I think if you see them campaign together in Florida and Ohio and other key swing states, people will feel better about it," he said. "They'll say, 'If she can get over it, why can't I?'"

[Clinton] reaffirmed her role in making political history as the first woman to come close to winning a presidential nomination.

"Although we weren't able to shatter that highest, hardest glass ceiling this time, thanks to you, it's got about 18 million cracks in it," she told her supporters.

Clinton appeared upbeat.

"This isn't exactly the party I planned, but I sure like company," she joked at the start of the 30-minute speech. ●

Elise Victoria, Ed Miller, Martin Truesdale, and Tyler Brown plant a tree in a vacant lot in east Baltimore while working for Civic Works.

Maryland

Total population   5,618,344

State population rank   19th

Median household income

Md.	**$68,080**
USA	**$50,740**

Race/ethnicity (as % of total pop.)

White **63.6%**

2.0% Other

5.0% Asian

29.5% Black

Non-Hispanic **94%**

Hispanic **6%**

10 Electoral votes

2004 general election result

✔ Kerry (D) **56%**

Bush (R) **43%**

2008 primary winners

✔ Obama (D)

✔ McCain (R)

Party strength	**D**	**R**
Governor	✔	
Senators	✔✔	
Representatives	6	2

Maryland feels pinch of thinning federal dollars

Both McCain and Obama promise help

By John Fritze • Excerpt from Tuesday, September 23, 2008 • BALTIMORE

Where Anthony Hurt once saw rubble and litter, he now sees a bright mural. From his second-story window, the view of drugs and decay has given way to sunflowers and trees.

More than 150 formerly vacant lots in this city, which is often derided for its high rate of violent crime, have been transformed into community parks—in part with the help of federal grants.

"It's what most neighborhoods need, instead of a dead lot," says Hurt, 52, who lives across the street from the new park. "It helps bring back up the neighborhood."

Urban governments rely on federal grants to pay for job training, police and even community parks. But many grant programs have been deeply cut in recent years, forcing local governments to find the money elsewhere or forgo services.

Reductions have hit especially hard in Baltimore, Maryland's largest city, which had 282 homicides last year, according to FBI statistics. The Census Bureau estimates that about 20% of Baltimore residents live in poverty.

"We rely heavily on those grants to revitalize neighborhoods and communities, to create opportunities for citizens," says Baltimore Mayor Sheila Dixon, a Democrat. "Over the last eight years ... we've lost a great deal of grant money."

Party enrollment figures favor Democrats 2-to-1 in Maryland, giving Democratic presidential nominee Barack Obama a significant advantage over Republican nominee John McCain. Both candidates have voiced support for grant programs that would help this state's poorest communities.

Obama would "roll back" cuts made to some programs, according to a campaign statement that offered few specifics about what he believes is an appropriate level of spending. McCain's campaign says the Republican would focus more attention on especially needy neighborhoods while reducing administrative costs.

Maryland has lost money in 85 grant categories since 2005, according to data provided by the Maryland Department of Budget and Management. ●

Obama is handed a sunflower by a supporter while on the campaign trail visiting the Greensboro Curb Market, a fruit and vegetable market in Greensboro, North Carolina.

North Carolina

Total population   9,061,032
State population rank   10th
Median household income

XXX	**$44,670**
USA	**$50,740**

Race/ethnicity (as % of total pop.)

White
74%

2.4% Other
1.9% Asian
21.7% Black

Non-Hispanic	**93%**
Hispanic	**7%**

15   Electoral votes

2004 general election result
✔ Bush (R)   **56%**
   Kerry (D)   **44%**

2008 primary winners
✔ Obama (D)
✔ McCain (R)

Party strength

	D	R
Governor	✔	
Senators		✔ ✔
Representatives	7	6

Military issues drive vote in N.C.

State's economy gets boost from its five bases

By Jordan Schrader • Excerpt from Friday, September 19, 2008 • JACKSONVILLE

L iving near the Marine Corps' largest base and watching new houses and schools going up to hold military families, Roger Denoncourt doesn't feel much of the economic pressure that is defining the 2008 presidential election.

The retired Marine says his vote will go to candidates he sees as supportive of the military.

Voters across the USA will go to the polls Nov. 4. They will consider the military debate that has divided the nation as they choose between Democrat Barack Obama, who has opposed the Iraq war from the start, and Republican John McCain, who backed it, favored sending more troops and argues for keeping them in Iraq for the long haul.

In North Carolina, home to five military bases, the question has added significance.

Leaving Iraq would risk thwarting gains in security, says Denoncourt, 57, after shopping at a Kmart near Camp Lejeune.

"I think that would be the biggest mistake America's ever made, to pull out. We're the world leader—and we need to be the leader—and we went over there to help the world, not just America."

One hundred miles up N.C. Highway 24, a former soldier buying gloves at a pawn shop near Fort Bragg expressed doubt.

"It's a lot of people getting killed over there," says Clarence Smith, a veteran of the 1989 Panama invasion, "and you tend to wonder: How far do we go?"

News of deployments and casualties "certainly elevates military affairs high into the consciousness of North Carolina voters," says Ferrel Guillory, director of the Program on Public Life at the University of North Carolina-Chapel Hill.

Long tours of duty have put stress on families and fostered doubts about the war, even in a place with a conservative, patriotic bent, Guillory says.

"My sense of it is support for the war, support for the president has tanked in this state, but not as much as it's tanked nationally," Guillory says.

An average of state polls taken Sept. 6-14 by the website RealClearPolitics puts McCain up 51% to 42% over Obama. ●

Governor Jon Corzine stumps for Obama at Rutgers University in New Brunswick, New Jersey.

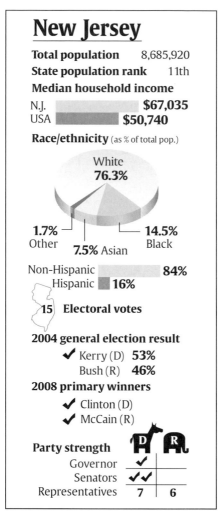

New Jersey

Total population   8,685,920

State population rank   11th

Median household income

N.J. **$67,035**

USA **$50,740**

Race/ethnicity (as % of total pop.)

White **76.3%**

1.7% Other

7.5% Asian

14.5% Black

Non-Hispanic **84%**

Hispanic **16%**

15   **Electoral votes**

2004 general election result

✔ Kerry (D) **53%**

Bush (R) **46%**

2008 primary winners

✔ Clinton (D)

✔ McCain (R)

Party strength	D	R
Governor	✔	
Senators	✔✔	
Representatives	7	6

N.J. governor puts business background to use

Obama campaign consults Corzine for economic advice

By Gregory J. Volpe • Excerpt from Friday, October 24, 2008 • TRENTON

Gov. Jon Corzine apparently has yet to convince a lot of New Jersey residents that he has the financial expertise to fix the state's economic problems.

Despite his success as chief executive of global investment firm Goldman Sachs in the 1990s, a Monmouth University-Gannett statewide poll conducted Oct. 15-18 found 47% rated his financial expertise as either "poor" or "only fair."

Nevertheless, Corzine has been serving as an economic spokesman for Democratic presidential candidate Barack Obama on national television programs and at campaign rallies in key battleground states.

"He's a guy…who has a deep breadth of knowledge about this stuff and can talk about it in a way that's pretty easy to un-

derstand for folks who aren't as knowledgeable about it as he is," says Andrew Poag, an Obama campaign spokesman on leave from Corzine's staff.

According to the Tax Foundation, a tax research organization based in Washington, D.C., New Jersey residents pay 11.8% of their income for state and local taxes—the nation's highest rate. That number has not improved since Corzine took office in 2006, foundation figures show.

"It's funny how he's become an expert on CNBC and we heard references made during the Democratic convention to good things that are happening in New Jersey, which certainly comes as a surprise to many New Jerseyans," Monmouth University pollster Patrick Murray says.

"If Obama really looked into what little Jon Corzine has done for the state, to me, it makes Obama's judgment more suspect," says David Fisher, 53, of Manasquan, N.J., a registered Republican and professional planner.

"People have confidence that we're thinking about the economy in a (sensible) way," Corzine counters. "Yes, correcting the problem comes with concerns, but it doesn't come with the abject failure that results from doing nothing, which is what has happened in Washington."

Tom Shea, Corzine's political adviser and former chief of staff, says whoever becomes president will parallel Corzine's path. "Making tough decisions to clean up problems that have appeared over a long time is not necessarily a recipe for popularity," Shea says. ●

Though New York may be the center of attention for a lot of things, it is not a huge factor in the 2008 presidential race.

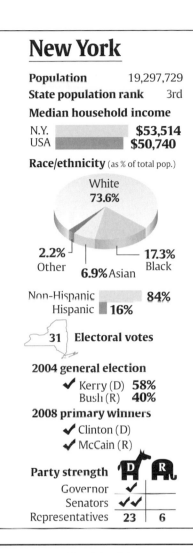

New York

Population   19,297,729

State population rank   3rd

Median household income

N.Y.	**$53,514**
USA	**$50,740**

Race/ethnicity (as % of total pop.)

White **73.6%**

2.2% Other

6.9% Asian

17.3% Black

Non-Hispanic **84%**

Hispanic **16%**

31   **Electoral votes**

2004 general election

✔ Kerry (D) **58%**

Bush (R) **40%**

2008 primary winners

✔ Clinton (D)

✔ McCain (R)

Party strength

	D	R
Governor	✔	
Senators	✔	✔
Representatives	23	6

In months, N.Y. politics go from red hot to ice cold

Battleground states getting "all the attention"

By Jay Gallagher • Excerpt from Tuesday, September 16, 2008 • ALBANY

"In presidential politics, New York's votes are already assigned," says Maurice Carroll, a former longtime New York City newspaper political reporter now doing polling on New York issues for Quinnipiac University in Connecticut. "So why should either Obama or McCain give much attention to New York, except for the money, except for the publicity?"

For New York, it used to be different.

For six successive presidential elections, from 1928 to 1948, at least one New Yorker was the presidential candidate of one of the major parties.

In 1944, two New Yorkers squared off: incumbent Democratic President (and former New York governor) Franklin D. Roosevelt and Republican Gov. Thomas E. Dewey.

Roosevelt, the only man ever elected president four times, was the sixth (and last) New Yorker to be president. He died in office in April 1945.

In 1948, Dewey seemed likely to make it five presidential wins in a row for New Yorkers, but he managed to blow a big lead to Democrat Harry Truman.

In those days, "New York was a leader with both parties because its demographic and population characteristics converged with the national demographic and population characteristics," says State University of New York-New Paltz Vice President Gerald Benjamin, the leading academic expert on New York government and politics.

As the country became more suburban and the South and West surged, New York became less important, he says.

"There's no doubt New York has lost some of its luster," says Gov. David Paterson, the former lieutenant governor who got the top job when Spitzer left.

The rest of the country seemed less tolerant of the sometimes boisterous, aggressive attitude of many New Yorkers, some of whom in turn resented the shift.

"New York seems to get lost in the shuffle sometimes," says Kandi Desrosiers, 43, from Rensselaer, N.Y.

Tara Golden of Albany, 28, concurs.

"Democrats always get the New York vote," she says. "I'm a Republican, so I don't really care about Hillary Clinton, (but) I think Giuliani would have been good." ●

Behind GOP ticket: Oklahoma County GOP Chairwoman Pam Pollard sizes up cutouts of John McCain and Sarah Palin.

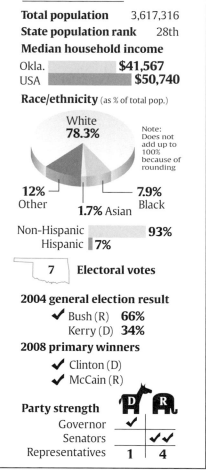

Oklahoma

Total population   3,617,316
State population rank   28th
Median household income
Okla.   **$41,567**
USA   **$50,740**

Race/ethnicity (as % of total pop.)

White
78.3%

Note: Does not add up to 100% because of rounding

12%
Other

1.7% Asian

7.9%
Black

Non-Hispanic   **93%**
Hispanic   **7%**

7   **Electoral votes**

2004 general election result
✔ Bush (R)   **66%**
Kerry (D)   **34%**

2008 primary winners
✔ Clinton (D)
✔ McCain (R)

Party strength

	D	R
Governor	✔	
Senators		✔✔
Representatives	1	4

Oklahoma holds tough times at bay, stands firmly Republican

A prosperous economy keeps Oklahomans happy with status quo

By Rick Jervis • Excerpt from Tuesday, October 21, 2008 • OKLAHOMA CITY

It's hard to feel the economic pinch rattling the rest of the country in the marble-floored halls of the Penn Square Mall in this city.

Shoppers carry overstuffed bags from Macy's, J. Crew and Build-A-Bear Workshop. Hungry visitors lunch at a "sushi station" in the middle of a bustling food court. Money flows from wallets to chain-store registers.

Thanks to the recent energy boom, life outside the mall is equally good. Unemployment in the state is at 4%, according to the federal Bureau of Labor Statistics—one of the lowest rates in the nation—and house values are actually going up.

But Oklahomans have seen such good times turn bad before.

Economic turmoil "hasn't gotten to us yet. But we know it will," says Jeff Bingham, 42, an accountant and registered Republican.

When voters here speak their mind on Nov. 4, that voice is expected to be resoundingly Republican. In a survey taken Oct. 4-5, by TVPoll.com, John McCain showed a staggering 37-point lead over Barack Obama.

Despite a Democratic governor and rifts among local Republican leaders, Oklahoma remains staunchly Republican, fueled by government mistrust and a politically active evangelical Christian base—estimated at about 57% of the electorate—says Keith Gaddie, a University of Oklahoma political science professor.

Oklahomans' distrust of government and corporations is rooted in the Dust Bowl years of the Great Depression, the oil bust of the 1980s and the more recent flight of corporations such as Halliburton and Conoco, he says.

"Big, private institutions leave Oklahoma," Gaddie says. "And government makes promises and doesn't deliver."

A desire for less government and lower taxes will pull most of the state toward McCain, says Oklahoma City Mayor Mick Cornett, a Republican. Obama is viewed as too liberal and too willing to bolster government programs to stand a chance, he says.

"People in Oklahoma don't wake up every morning wondering what the government is going to do for them," he says. ●

Red vote turns blue: "We need change," Ron Booth says in Houston. He voted Republican in 2004 but plans to back Barack Obama.

Texas

Total population   23,904,380

State population rank   2nd

Median household income

Texas	**$47,548**
USA	**$50,740**

Race/ethnicity (as % of total pop.)

White **82.6%**

Note: Does not add up to 100% because of rounding

2.1% Other

3.4% Asian

12% Black

Non-Hispanic	**64%**
Hispanic	**36%**

34   **Electoral votes**

2004 general election result

✔ Bush (R)   **61%**
  Kerry (D)   **38%**

2008 primary/caucus winners

✔ Clinton[1] (D)/Obama[2] (D)
✔ McCain[1] (R)

1 – Primary; 2 – Caucus

Party strength

	D	R
Governor		✔
Senators		✔✔
Representatives	13	19

Hurricanes may help steer Texas politics

Subtle shifts afoot, from an influx of Katrina Dems to Ike-affected campaigns

By Rick Jervis • Excerpt from Wednesday, October 22, 2008 • HOUSTON

Ron Booth voted Republican in the presidential election four years ago. In the staunchly Republican state of Texas, home to President Bush, that's not much of a surprise. Booth says, however, that in November, he'll cast his vote for the Democratic presidential candidate, Sen. Barack Obama.

"You can't do the things of the past to solve the problems of the future," says Booth, 45, a finance manager, as he lunched recently at an outdoor cafe in downtown Houston. "We need change. That's Obama, clearly."

Some areas long considered Republican strongholds, such as Dallas County, are rapidly turning purple and may be all-out blue by November. 5.

Texas' 34 electoral votes most likely will go to McCain, says Jim Henson, who directs the Texas Politics Project at the University of Texas-Austin. But a national fervor for change, especially opposing the Bush administration, is seeping into Texas, he says.

"Republicans have had the keys to the cars the last 10 years," Henson says, "but over the last two to four years, there's been ... disaffection with the way Washington has governed and the way Texas has governed. There's a sense that Republicans have failed to deliver on issues."

Few places will be more closely watched than Harris County, which includes Houston, the USA's fourth-largest city, and has been a stalwart GOP county.

The outcome in this area, recently battered by Hurricane Ike, could reveal what post-Bush Texas politics will look like.

Urban flight, a growing minority population and an influx of Katrina Democrats from Louisiana have contributed to the shifting mood in urban centers such as Dallas, Republican strategist Chris Turner says.

Those demographic shifts don't readily apply to Harris County, he says. Ike's destruction in the coastal areas may have hurt the Democrats because it was hard for candidates to reach those areas, he says. ●

A Maricopa Sheriff's Deputy detains Armando Garcia, 18, after he admitted to not having the proper identification to be in the country.

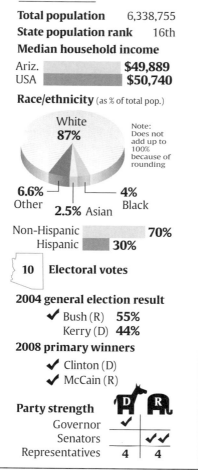

Arizona

Total population 6,338,755

State population rank 16th

Median household income

Ariz. **$49,889**
USA **$50,740**

Race/ethnicity (as % of total pop.)

White
87%

Note: Does not add up to 100% because of rounding

6.6% Other
2.5% Asian
4% Black

Non-Hispanic **70%**
Hispanic **30%**

10 | **Electoral votes**

2004 general election result
✔ Bush (R) **55%**
Kerry (D) **44%**

2008 primary winners
✔ Clinton (D)
✔ McCain (R)

Party strength

	D	**R**
Governor	✔	
Senators		✔✔
Representatives	4	4

Immigration still a "political hot potato" in Ariz.

Presidential candidates have been silent on issue

By Dennis Wagner • Excerpt from Friday, October 24, 2008 • PHOENIX

While some of Arizona's key political races this year are dominated by illegal immigration, the issue has virtually disappeared from the presidential campaigns and debates.

Republican Sen. John McCain, who championed a comprehensive immigration overhaul bill three years ago, has barely addressed the topic even though it remains a hot-button controversy in his home state. Democratic Sen. Barack Obama, who also supports an overhaul, has been nearly as mum.

During three presidential debates, the word "immigration" was uttered only once, according to a check of transcripts posted online by the Commission on Presidential Debates. In that one instance, McCain accused Obama of misrepresenting McCain's position on the topic. There was no further discussion.

By contrast, Maricopa County Sheriff Joe Arpaio seeks re-election in the Phoenix metro area based largely on his effort to round up and deport illegal immigrants—an enforcement program condemned by Hispanic leaders and Mayor Phil Gordon as "racial profiling."

Arpaio is the top law officer in a county that, at 9,200 square miles, is bigger than New Jersey, and has a larger population — 3.8 million—than half of the states.

The sheriff mocks both presidential candidates for dodging the issue: "Where did it go? Why is it off the radar?" he says. "I'm not an expert on politics, but I think it has to do with (getting) the Hispanic vote."

"It's a political hot potato," says Elias Bermudez, founder and chairman of a Phoenix-based advocacy group called Immigrants Without Borders. "They don't want to touch it because it will alienate their base in both parties."

Bermudez, a McCain supporter, notes that both candidates have endorsed a potential pathway to citizenship for the estimated 12 million illegal immigrants in the USA, a program reviled as "amnesty" by conservatives.

Obama might lose undecided voters if he speaks out against Arpaio, Bermudez says, and McCain would lose staunch conservatives; so the strategy is silent disapproval. ●

John Barbour demonstrates how to make wooden bourbon barrels at the Kentucky Bourbon Festival in Bardstown.

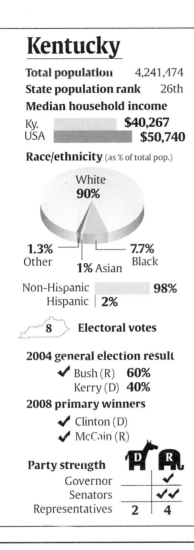

Kentucky

Total population 4,241,474

State population rank 26th

Median household income

Ky. $40,267
USA $50,740

Race/ethnicity (as % of total pop.)

White **90%**

1.3% Other
1% Asian
7.7% Black

Non-Hispanic **98%**
Hispanic **2%**

8 Electoral votes

2004 general election result
✔ Bush (R) **60%**
Kerry (D) **40%**

2008 primary winners
✔ Clinton (D)
✔ McCain (R)

Party strength	D	R
Governor		✔
Senators		✔✔
Representatives	2	4

Kentucky "does not fit on...left-right scales"

McCain holds big lead; other races are closer

By Jessie Halladay • Excerpt from Monday, September 29, 2008 • BARDSTOWN

Kentucky has not made the list of battleground states in this year's presidential election, but that hasn't dampened interest for Kentuckians who say this election is one of the most important they've seen in years.

"I'm 51, and I've heard more talk this year than I ever have," says John Barbour of New Haven.

At last week's Kentucky Bourbon Festival here, south of Louisville, Barbour demonstrated how to make the wooden bourbon barrels he produces for Kentucky Cooperage. He and other voters stopped to talk about what's important to them in this presidential election.

"I want to know what they think about the guy who's up every morning with a lunchbox in a pickup truck and rolling," Barbour says.

Many people here say the issues they are thinking about mirror those of other states: the economy, the war in Iraq and gas prices.

"What's happening nationally—people losing their homes, their jobs—it's happening here," says John Payne, 53, a distillery worker who lives in Bardstown.

Kelvin Elam of Lebanon says his concerns over gas prices and the housing market have prompted him to register to vote after skipping all elections for 12 years.

"I'm really concerned about my children being able to buy a home and, if they did, to be able to keep it," says Elam, 46, a surgical technician student. "If we don't get involved, we're just going to get in worse shape."

Since 1964, when Lyndon Johnson was elected, Kentucky has always cast its electoral votes for the winning presidential candidate.

Stephen Voss, a political science professor at the University of Kentucky, says he expects voter turnout in the commonwealth to be high, despite the fact that it is not considered a player in the national election.

"The average Kentuckian is having the usual difficulties of our pocketbooks taking us one way and our values taking us another way," Voss says. "Kentucky does not fit on the classic left-right scales." ●

Mark Vetsch, owner of Mr. Mark Music in Anoka, Minnesota, adjusts a bass guitar. In 2007 Anoka County had 1,848 foreclosures, the highest rate in the St. Paul metro area.

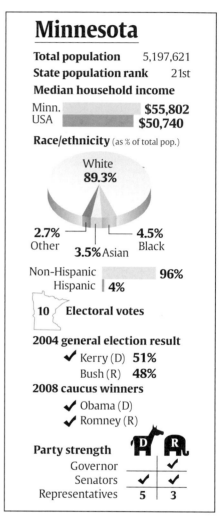

Minnesota

Total population 5,197,621
State population rank 21st
Median household income
Minn. **$55,802**
USA **$50,740**

Race/ethnicity (as % of total pop.)

White **89.3%**

2.7% Other
3.5% Asian
4.5% Black

Non-Hispanic **96%**
Hispanic **4%**

10 **Electoral votes**

2004 general election result
✔ Kerry (D) **51%**
Bush (R) **48%**

2008 caucus winners
✔ Obama (D)
✔ Romney (R)

Party strength	D	R
Governor		✔
Senators	✔	✔
Representatives	5	3

Minnesotans abuzz over Senate race

Voters have ballot smorgasbord with three candidates in ring

By Judy Keen • Excerpt from Tuesday, October 28, 2008 • ANOKA

The hottest campaign here this year pits a veteran Republican politician against a Democratic newcomer and has people debating the need for change and which candidate can help fix the economy.

It's not the presidential race between John McCain and Barack Obama that has people in this Minneapolis suburb buzzing. It's the close, costly and contentious U.S. Senate contest between Republican incumbent Norm Coleman and Democrat Al Franken, a comedian, writer and first-time candidate.

A few months ago, Franken faced questions about his entertainment company's unpaid taxes and his campaign seemed stalled, says Larry Jacobs, director of the Center for the Study of Politics and Governance at the University of Minnesota.

Growing economic worries changed that, he says. "Franken has been surfing the bad news in America, and his campaign has really got that anti-Republican wind in its sails," Jacobs says.

Over lunch at Legal Grounds, a downtown coffee shop, Jeff Christopher, 66, a retired carpenter, and his daughter Aleesha Ackerman, 32, a secretary, say they usually disagree on politics. He's inclined to support Republicans, and she leans to Democrats. Concern about the economy, though, has both of them planning to vote for Franken.

"Everybody's talking about the economy because it's right in their living room," Ackerman says. Salaries at the RV dealership where her mother-in-law works were just cut in half, and Ackerman worries about her own job. Franken, she says, "seems more in touch with people who are struggling." Her dad adds, "He's going to listen to the people."

At a nearby table, sheriff's detectives Edward Egly, 53, and Larry Johnson, 44, say they will vote for Coleman. "I'm not going to throw a senior senator out because a guy moves here from New York and decides to run," Egly says. The economy is important, he says, but so is national security, and he agrees with Coleman's tough stance on terrorism. Franken's family moved to Minnesota when he was 4, and he returned to the state in 2005. ●

Obama, center, appears on stage with Virginia Governor Timothy M. Kaine, left, and Senate candidate, former Gov. Mark Warner, right, during a rally at the James Madison University Convocation Center.

Virginia

Total population   7,712,091

State population rank   12th

Median household income

Va.	**$59,562**
USA	**$50,740**

Race/ethnicity (as % of total pop.)

White **73.2%**

2.1% Other
4.8% Asian
19.9% Black

Non-Hispanic **93%**
Hispanic **7%**

13   **Electoral votes**

2004 general election result

✔ Bush (R)   **54%**
  Kerry (D)   **45%**

2008 primary winners

✔ Obama (D)
✔ McCain (R)

Party strength

	D	**R**
Governor	✔	
Senators	✔	✔
Representatives	3	8

Democrats have sights on Va. as battleground

Voting patterns have shifted, but southern region is solidly GOP

By Alan Gomez • Excerpt from Monday, September 22, 2008 • MECHANICSVILLE

Gordon Maddox, a retired career police officer in this southern Virginia town, ticked off his priorities when deciding who to vote for in a presidential race.

"Integrity." "Good moral character." "Christian leadership."

These qualities rarely appear in national polls asking voters to list their priorities this election. But they come up often in southern Virginia, home to numerous military schools and evangelical universities.

Largely on the strength of this region, Republicans have been taking Virginia in presidential elections for decades. The last time a Democrat won here was in 1964 when Lyndon Johnson defeated U.S. Sen. Barry Goldwater.

But Democrats believe the political stars may be aligned to turn the Old Dominion their way.

For instance, Virginia has elected back-to-back Democrats for governor. In 2006, voters sent a Democrat to the U.S. Senate to replace a Republican. And Democrats made significant gains in 2007 in the Virginia House and took control of the state Senate.

Most important, Democrats may not have to win over southern Virginians.

That's because the Virginia counties in the north close to Washington, D.C., have seen a huge influx of people in recent years and they vote Democratic.

"Northern Virginia has gotten deeper and deeper blue," says Bob Hovis, 66, a

lawyer who lives in Fairfax County about 15 miles from Washington. "I think this is the year to turn Virginia completely blue."

Since 2004, one out of every four new voter registrations have been in three counties: Fairfax, Loudoun and Prince William, according to figures from the state Board of Elections. All are in Northern Virginia.

Mark Rozell, a public policy professor based at George Mason University's Arlington campus, says he had expected the growth of the Democrat-leaning north and an increase in minority groups (which tend to vote Democratic) around the state to eventually weaken the Republican grip. But the change "came about more suddenly and dramatically than I had ever imagined." ●

Every volunteer counts: First-time voters and volunteers Natalie Zamora and Greg Montoya-Mora, both 18, walk the Far Northeast Heights area of Albuquerque canvassing for the McCain campaign.

New Mexico

Total population   1,969,915

State population rank   36th

Median household income

N.M.	**$41,452**
USA	**$50,740**

Race/ethnicity (as % of total pop.)

White **84.5%**

11.3% Other   **1.4%** Asian   **2.8%** Black

Non-Hispanic **56%**
Hispanic **44%**

5   Electoral votes

2004 general election result

✔ Bush (R)   **50%**
Kerry (D)   **49%**

2008 caucus/primary winners

✔ Clinton[1] (D)
✔ McCain [2] (R)

1 – Caucus; 2 – Primary

Party strength   D   R

	D	R
Governor	✔	
Senators	✔	✔
Representatives	1	2

N.M. teams realize every vote counts

State sees flurry of volunteers working to mobilize supporters

By **John Fritze** • Excerpt from Thursday, October 23, 2008 • ALBUQUERQUE

In this battleground state, Jennifer Chadwell-Feld is at war. Chadwell-Feld, 58, dials voters from a small warehouse, gauging support for Republican presidential nominee John McCain and reminding them a vote Nov. 4 could be crucial in one of the nation's tightest swing states.

"Since you support McCain, would you be willing to volunteer for the campaign?" the volunteer says and records the answers, which will be entered into a computer. "Can we get you a yard sign?"

In New Mexico, where President Bush eked out a win in 2004 by fewer than 6,000 votes, the race between McCain and Democrat Barack Obama may depend as much on volunteers as any stump speech or television ad by the candidates.

"We're seeing intense mobilization efforts," says Lonna Atkeson, a political science professor at the University of New Mexico. "We've already had a lot of early voting turnout."

Energized by the idea that every vote may count, Jesse Cresdin, 21, an Obama volunteer, moves quickly through a neighborhood in Las Vegas, N.M. Obama is the first candidate he can recall opening an office in town, he says.

"We're making sure that everybody ... is registered to vote," Cresdin, clipboard in hand, tells Alfred Marquez, 31, before handing him an "Obamanos" sticker, a play on Obama's name and the Spanish word vamonos, "let's go."

Even a slim advantage could be key in New Mexico, which supported Bush in 2004 but Al Gore—by 366 votes—in 2000.

In 2004, Bush rallied voters in rural portions of the state, says Joe Monahan, who runs joemonahan.com, a political blog. That effort helped Republicans offset gains Democrats made in Albuquerque and other cities. This year, Monahan says, McCain is taking a similar path. "If he's going to win New Mexico, he's going to try to do it the same way George Bush did, a surge in the south," he says. ●

Voters drop off their voter registration forms at the Multnomah County Elections Office on October 14, 2008, in Portland.

Oregon

Total population   3,747,455

State population rank   27th

Median household income

Ore.		**$48,730**
USA		**$50,740**

Race/ethnicity (as % of total pop.)

White **90.3%**

Note: Does not add up to 100% because of rounding

4.1% Other

3.7% Asian

2.0% Black

Non-Hispanic **89%**

Hispanic **11%**

7   Electoral votes

2004 general election result

✔ Kerry (D) **51%**

Bush (R) **47%**

2008 primary winners

✔ Obama (D)

✔ McCain (R)

Party strength

	D	R
Governor	✔	
Senators	✔	✔
Representatives	4	1

ELECTIONS

AP Images

Oregon not really "in play" this time

Neither nominee visits as state considered locked in for Obama

By Tracy Loew • Excerpt from Tuesday, October 28, 2008 • SALEM

G reg Fabos has been a campaign volunteer since supporting Eugene McCarthy for president 40 years ago. He says this is the most electric battle for the White House he's ever seen.

"I think people here are seeing that the country is in trouble, and they're ready to vote for change," the 66-year-old marketing consultant says.

The energy Fabos says he senses comes in spite of the fact that Oregon, for the first time in years, is being snubbed by the presidential contenders.

Neither candidate has made an Oregon campaign appearance.

"Oregon really is not in play," says Bill Lunch, chairman of Oregon State University's political science department.

While Oregon hasn't voted for a Republican president since choosing Ronald Reagan in 1984, it was considered a swing state in the past two elections, says Jim Moore, who teaches political science at Pacific University in Forest Grove, Ore.

This time around, Lunch says, the state was in play until candidate John McCain's bounce from the Republican National Convention faded in mid-September. According to a Rasmussen Reports poll conducted Oct. 14, Democratic nominee Barack Obama is leading McCain 54% to 41%.

"The Republicans have been having trouble in Oregon ever since 2000," Lunch says. "Step by step, the state has been getting bluer."

Both campaigns, however, insist they are not taking the state for granted.

Rick Gorka, regional spokesman for the McCain campaign, calls the campaign in Oregon "very grass-roots."

"We're doing the door-to-door and phone banking that's necessary to win in November," he says.

The Obama campaign has 14 field offices across the state, Obama campaign spokeswoman Sahar Wali says. The campaign focused mostly on voter registration until the Oct. 14 registration deadline, Wali says, and now is encouraging people to vote early.

Despite the lack of attention, Oregon has set a voter-registration record this year. According to the secretary of State's office, 2.17 million are registered to vote—an increase of just over 25,000 from the previous record of 2.14 million, set for the 2004 elections. ●

"Time to change America"

Obama offers details on taxes, energy and defense

By Kathy Kiely and William M. Welch • Excerpt from Friday, August 29, 2008 • DENVER

Sen. Barack Obama, speaking on the fourth and final night of the convention.

With a display of fireworks and pageantry worthy of an Olympic opening, Barack Obama began his historic campaign as the Democratic presidential nominee Thursday. He promised to reform Washington's "broken politics" and attacked his Republican rival John McCain as a clone of President Bush.

"America, we are better than these last eight years," Obama said.

Against the backdrop of the Rocky Mountains, Obama accepted the nomination in a packed outdoor football stadium. That followed an example set by John Kennedy, and allowed Obama to open up the convention finale to an enthusiastic crowd estimated at 84,000 in a traditionally Republican state he hopes to win this November.

Obama is the first African American to capture a major party's presidential nomination. His remarks—coming 45 years to the day after civil rights leader Martin Luther King Jr. outlined his vision of racial equality—touched on his historic role in politics.

"I realize that I am not the likeliest candidate for this office," Obama said. "I don't fit the typical pedigree."

He said his ascent to the threshold of the White House symbolizes "that promise that has always set this country apart."

He paid tribute to his late mother, Stanley Ann, "who once turned to food stamps" to support him, and to his grandmother, Madelyn Dunham, too frail to travel from Hawaii. "She's the one who put off buying a new car or a new dress for herself so that I could have a better life," he said.

Appearing shortly after 10 p.m. ET to a thunderous roar in Invesco Field, Obama made his case that he and running mate Sen. Joe Biden of Delaware are more in tune with the needs of average Americans than McCain. "We measure progress by how many people can find a job that pays the mortgage," Obama told the cheering crowd.

His speech outlined plans to cut taxes for middle-income earners and small businesses, promote alternative energy sources and help the auto industry revamp its assembly lines "so that the fuel-

More than 84,000 people packed into Invesco Field in Denver to witness Obama's acceptance of the Democratic presidential nomination.

efficient cars of the future are built right here in America."

Obama paid tribute to McCain's record as a Vietnam POW, saying he served "with bravery and distinction." But he leveled sharp criticisms at the Arizona senator, saying McCain "stands alone in his stubborn refusal to end a misguided war" and that "he has been anything but independent" of Bush.

McCain spokesman Tucker Bounds called Obama's speech "misleading."

There was an early indication that the convention helped Obama, who began the week even with McCain in the Gallup daily tracking poll but who leaves Denver with a six-point lead.

Obama's moment came as McCain was preparing to unveil his vice presidential pick today and considering a delay of next week's GOP national convention because of a hurricane threatening New Orleans—almost three years after Hurricane Katrina devastated the city and the slow federal response damaged Bush's popularity. ●

In Biden, a life story to complement Obama's

Delaware senator could help lure working class, Clinton supporters

By Jill Lawrence and Martha T. Moore • Excerpt from Monday, August 25, 2008 • DENVER

(above) Vice Presidential Nominee Sen. Joe Biden, D-Del, addresses the Democratic National Convention in Denver, Wednesday, Aug. 27, 2008. (opposite) Biden, Obama and their families salute the crowd at Invesco Field.

Maybe you didn't know that Joe Biden stuttered as a kid, takes a 91-minute train ride home to his wife each night and is so well known in a must-win swing state he's been called "Pennsylvania's third senator."

Barack Obama tapped as his running mate a man whose dramatic life story rivals his own, and holds political appeal far beyond the foreign-policy expertise that is Biden's most obvious asset.

The Delaware senator balances this ticket in many other ways. With his working-class background, Biden could help Obama fight his portrayal as a candidate of the elites, and win over the women voters who passionately supported Hillary Rodham Clinton. He's 65 years old to Obama's 47, Catholic to Obama's Protestant. Unlike Obama, he didn't attend Ivy League schools.

Though Obama has frustrated some Democrats by being slow to attack, Biden is blunt and eager to wage political combat—qualities that could allow Obama to remain above the fray. Biden, who overcame his stutter as a boy by relentless drills, is a gifted if sometimes windy speaker who goes for the gut.

"He's comfortable on the attack and that will serve the ticket well," says Rep. Artur Davis, D-Ala.

Biden also stays close to his roots—in his visits to his hometown of Scranton, Pa., in the laws he works to pass and in the allies he's made in Delaware politics. When he returned last week from a trip to the embattled Republic of Georgia, for instance, he headed straight from the airport to a promised appearance at a firefighters hall.

In choosing Biden, Obama essentially is calculating that the Delaware senator's penchant for occasional gaffes won't be a distraction in the fall campaign.

Biden was driven from the 1988 presidential race for failing to credit a British politician for a passage Biden used in a stump speech. Biden has been lambasted more recently for clumsily praising Obama as "clean" and "articulate" and saying that in Delaware "you cannot go to a 7-Eleven or a Dunkin' Donuts unless you have a

slight Indian accent." Hours after Obama made his pick, Republicans launched a "Biden gaffe clock."

The same brain-to-mouth quickness that sometimes misfires, on the other hand, produced possibly the most memorable and cutting line of the primary season: Biden's contention that every sentence uttered by former New York mayor Rudy Giuliani—at the time a candidate for the GOP nomination—was "a noun, a verb and 9/11."

Pennsylvania Gov. Ed Rendell, another Democrat whose bluntness sometimes gets him in trouble, cast Biden's misfires as endearing. "It's pretty easy to fall in love with Joe Biden," he told USA TODAY Sunday.

"Even his mistakes, you have a tendency to shake your head and say, 'But that's Joe.' "

Another potential downside of Obama's pick is one of the reasons he made it: the weight of Biden's experience. It's reassuring to wavering voters worried about Obama's short national resume. But it could undercut Obama's message of change.

Republicans have seized on that line of attack. Minnesota Gov. Tim Pawlenty, a Republican often mentioned as a possible running mate for John McCain, on Sunday called Biden a "consummate insider" who was elected to the Senate when he and Obama were 11. "And he's known as being long-winded on top of that," Pawlenty

added on a Republican party conference call. "Where's the change?"

Obama concluded the benefits outweigh the risks.

"Mostly, I think what attracted Sen. Obama was Biden's wisdom," senior strategist David Axelrod said on ABC's This Week. "And not the kind of wisdom you get in Washington, D.C., but the kind of wisdom you get when you overcome adversity, tragedy in your life as he has; the kind of wisdom you get in the working-class communities of Scranton, Pa., and Wilmington, Del."

Tragedy struck early for Biden. Shortly after he was elected to the Senate at age 29,

his wife and young daughter were killed in a car crash as they shopped for a Christmas tree; his two young sons were badly injured.

In an emotional speech to the International Association of Fire Fighters last year, a shirt-sleeved Biden described his debt to his local firefighters. "My firefighters saved my children," he said.

In 1988, Biden had a life-threatening aneurysm and local firefighters again raced to the rescue. "I would not have lived" but for them, he told the group.

"We owe you big," he said. "You took care of me in the worst time of my life."

Biden was persuaded to take office as planned in January 1973 and, with his sister helping him look after his sons during the day, commuted home to see his recovering little boys every night. That set a pattern that has continued throughout his second marriage to Jill Jacobs in 1977.

The older of his two sons, Beau, 39, says that makes Joe Biden an outside-the-Beltway candidate. He became an Amtrak regular for more than three decades so he could "be home at my ballgames and be at the dinner table," Beau Biden told USA TODAY last year.

Appeal to women

Though Obama leads McCain 48%-42% among women in a USA TODAY/Gallup Poll released Sunday, Biden's family life and his legislative record on women's issues could help win disappointed fans of Hillary Rodham Clinton and enlarge that gender gap.

Working Mother magazine said Sunday that Biden is one of 24 lawmakers on its "2008 Best of Congress" list. "He puts kids' health, safety and education at the top of his priorities list," the magazine said. It said he has worked recently on a bill to reduce class size and "along with his wife, Jill, Biden has been a longtime leader in the fight against breast cancer."

Biden supports abortion rights and, as a senior member and former chairman of the Senate Judiciary Committee, has helped block anti-abortion jurists. Emily's List President Ellen Malcolm, whose group supports female abortion-rights candidates, called Biden "a passionate advocate for women" whose "commitment to family will resonate with women voters across this country."

When Biden was chairman of the Senate Judiciary Committee in 1991, some feminists alleged that he was too easy on

Senator Joe Biden, D-Del, holds his grandson, Hunter, after Biden's speech at the 2008 Democratic National Convention in Denver.

Supreme Court nominee Clarence Thomas and too hard on Anita Hill, a former co-worker of Thomas' who had accused the federal judge of sexual harassment. Three years later, however, Biden was praised by many feminists for what he calls one of his proudest accomplishments: writing the 1994 Violence Against Women Act.

Joseph Pika, a political scientist at the University of Delaware, says Biden was at least in part making amends. "He very self-consciously tried to shore up his support from women voters after the Anita Hill episode," he says.

He says Biden's "respectful" treatment of Clinton could help Obama with Clinton supporters who have been reluctant to come on board.

Republicans, however, are doing what they can to stoke lingering resentments. McCain has released a TV ad called "Passed Over," lamenting that Clinton was not chosen as Obama's running mate. Giuliani, speaking on ABC's This Week, said Clinton should have been "a no-brainer" for Obama.

It's unclear how many Clinton supporters remain offended. One prominent Clinton ally, Florida Rep. Debbie Wasserman Schultz, 42, switched to Obama right after the primaries and is even more enthusiastic now that Biden is on the ticket. She says she has been "an admirer of him for forever, gaffes and all," since her college days as a member of Students for Biden. "I had the button on my backpack and the whole deal."

Working class background

When Biden was named, Obama's Pennsylvania office put out a release headlined "Obama selects Pennsylvania's third senator." Delaware, south of Pennsylvania, is in the Philadelphia news media market. "People know him big time, and everything he does is reported by Philadelphia television," Rendell says.

What's more, Pennsylvania had Republican senators for 26 of the 30 years between 1977 and 2007—prompting some elected Democrats to turn to Biden for help. "He really handled Pennsylvania for us," says Rep. Paul Kanjorski, who represents the Scranton and Wilkes-Barre areas.

The strongest tie is Biden's abiding affection for Scranton, where he lived until he was 10. In the northeast corner of the state, Scranton is in the middle of swing-voter territory, home to working-class Catholic voters who in the Democratic primaries went solidly for Clinton.

Biden often invokes his blue-collar background with tales of his childhood playmates and uncles talking politics around the kitchen table, and he visits Scranton every year. Last year, he took his 91-year-old mother, Jean Finnegan, to visit the house where the family once lived.

"Scranton never leaves you; it's in your blood," Biden said in an interview published Sunday by the *Scranton Times-Tribune*. "I don't know, maybe I have a little romanticized view because I love the place so much."

He said his mother, who lives with him, kissed him as he left for Springfield, Ill., to be introduced as Obama's running mate. "Joey, everybody in Scranton'll be so proud," she told him.

The new USA TODAY/Gallup Poll shows Obama leading McCain 52%-36% among registered voters making less than $50,000 a year. Biden could help him solidify his standing in crucial states where he lost working-class voters badly to Clinton.

In northeastern Pennsylvania, Obama lost to Clinton 3 to 1. Kanjorski, who backed Clinton, says he has been worried about "stabilizing" his region for Obama. "Joe Biden goes 1,000 miles in that direction," he says. "He's a favorite son."

The Obama campaign is betting that Biden's blue-collar appeal will extend throughout the Rust Belt, and some political analysts agree. Alexander Lamis, a political scientist at Case Western Reserve University in Cleveland, says lower-income white voters will determine the election in those states. "Biden helps," he says. "He's plain-spoken and down-to-earth and will resonate in working-class areas."

Student of the world

As chairman of the Senate Foreign Relations Committee, Biden eases the minds of people who want seasoning along with change. Pawlenty, in talking points also pressed by Giuliani and on a new GOP website called NotReady08.com, said Biden's resume amounts to "overcompensation" for Obama's "lack of readiness" to be president.

"It's not a situation where you should have to have a mentor or a trainer or a superviser," he said.

Biden himself cited Obama's inexperience during the primary campaign, but made light of that in his interview with the Scranton newspaper. "Guess what, he got experienced real quick," Biden joked, then added: "I was running against him, man. What did they expect me to do, lean over and hug him and say, 'Yeah, he was the most experienced? He has plenty of experience?' Hey, man, the only thing I had going was experience."

One state where his experience could make a difference is Florida, with its large contingent of Jewish voters. Obama has rattled some Jewish voters because he is open to high-level dipomacy with Iran and because last year he told the American Israel Public Affairs Committee that "nobody is suffering more than the Palestinian people."

Wasserman Schultz, who represents the Fort Lauderdale area, says Biden is viewed as a strong supporter of Israel and his presence on the ticket will "go a long way to winning over" Jewish voters. She says she's been told Biden will campaign in Florida: "He has worked the condos. I have worked the condos with Joe Biden before in my district. People will be excited and fired up."

If the choice of Biden works the way Obama hopes, winning the White House would raise a question that Biden himself has brought up: Can he adapt to working for someone else?

Biden has been his own boss since he won an unexpected Senate victory in 1972. He has run his Senate office, the Senate Judiciary Committee and now the Senate Foreign Relations Committee. He has been set back on his heels personally and politically, but it hasn't broken his faith in himself and his talents.

"One of the hardest things for Joe Biden, should they win, will be to stand silently by the president. Vice presidents are seen but not heard," Pika says. "Verbal problems are probably controllable: He'll stay on message. (But) I think playing second fiddle is going to be tough for him." ●

"Fight for what's right"

McCain touts "record and scars," calls Obama a novice

By David Jackson • Excerpt from Friday, September 5, 2008 • ST. PAUL

Republican nominee John McCain greets the delegates at his acceptance speech Thursday night.

Republican John McCain launched the final phase of his presidential campaign against Barack Obama on Thursday, trumpeting a record of reform while casting his Democratic rival as unprepared for global leadership.

McCain, accepting his party's nomination, sought to claim Obama's campaign theme as his own. Along with running mate Sarah Palin, he said the GOP ticket has a "warning to the old, big-spending, do-nothing, me-first, country-second Washington crowd: Change is coming."

The Nov. 4 election will make history, producing either the first black president in Obama or the first female vice president in Palin, the governor of Alaska.

McCain praised Palin for tackling corruption and working with Democrats: "I can't wait until I introduce her to Washington."

Two anti-war hecklers were escorted out of the arena. "Don't be diverted by the ground noise and the static," McCain pleaded.

Running in a tough year for Republicans, McCain depicted himself as above party. To Obama, he said, "we'll go at it over the next two months," but "you have my respect and my admiration."

The four-term Arizona senator said he worked with Democrats on immigration and campaign-finance laws—and often drew flak from his party and has the "record and the scars to prove it. Sen. Obama does not."

Recalling his 5$^1/_2$ years as a Vietnam prisoner of war, McCain said he was transformed: "I wasn't my own man anymore. I was my country's."

McCain criticized Obama for opposing the 2007 increase of troops into Iraq and asserted that "the surge" has put the U.S. on the verge of victory.

Earlier in the day, Obama acknowledged on Fox News Channel that "the surge has succeeded in ways that nobody anticipated." However, he said Iraqi leaders "still haven't taken responsibility" for their country.

McCain and Palin greet the delegates at the Republican National Convention.

The speech ended with McCain's call to "fight for what's right for our country."

Colleen Chaney, an alternate delegate from Richmond, Ky., said she was brought to tears. McCain "not only showed his heart...but he also gave some really good specifics."

Obama spokesman Bill Burton said that McCain lashed out at Washington but that "he's been part of that crowd for 26 years."

McCain and Palin were off to Wisconsin after the speech for a tour of battleground states. The Gallup daily tracking poll showed Obama leading 49%–42%. ●

McCain's bet on Palin sets up a "wild ride" in fall campaign

Will the surprise pick lift him up or drag him down as new questions surface about her?

By Susan Page and Martha T. Moore • Excerpt from Wednesday, September 3, 2008 • ST. PAUL

(above) Republican nominee John McCain greets the delegates with his running mate, Sarah Palin. (opposite) Palin waves to the crowd at the XCEL Center in St. Paul, Minnesota.

Call it McCain's Gamble. The Republican presidential candidate is pulling bigger crowds and a gusher of cash to his campaign since his unexpected pick Friday of Alaska Gov. Sarah Palin as his running mate.

But questions about how rigorously John McCain vetted Palin and fresh scrutiny of the governor's record are fueling a larger debate about McCain's shoot-from-the-hip style and Palin's qualifications, in a crisis, to be president.

Can the first-term governor of a state with more caribou than people rescue the GOP in a tough election year?

Palin has the potential to shake up a race in which the field is tilted in the Democrats' favor by economic angst and a desire for change—or to be a disastrous distraction that makes McCain's course even steeper. The nine weeks from now until Election Day will determine whether she is "an enormous asset and a game-changer or she turns out to be a liability," says former House speaker Newt Gingrich.

"It's going to be a wild ride," he says.

For many Americans, Palin's speech tonight will be their first look at her. Written by former White House speechwriter Matt Scully, it will combine autobiography and policy.

"She's going to talk to the delegates about the future of this country, about how to reform broken institutions of government," says McCain strategist Steve Schmidt. "People will hear about her reform-and-change message" and about energy and its links to national security.

"She'll also communicate directly to the American people who she is," Schmidt says.

Her reception in the convention hall is sure to be positive, given the enthusiastic reaction she's received from delegates and other Republican activists so far. The McCain campaign raised $7 million

on Friday, the day Palin made her debut as running mate—its largest daily haul of the campaign. In rallies since in Ohio and Pennsylvania, McCain and Palin drew larger and more enthusiastic crowds than McCain usually draws alone.

However, it's clear that the GOP has a long way to go in selling Palin as a candidate to everyone else.

At a discussion Sunday with undecided voters from Minnesota, hosted by Republican pollster Frank Luntz, not one of the 25 participants thought Palin is currently qualified to be president. In a USA TODAY/Gallup Poll taken Friday, 51% said they had never heard of her. Six of 10 said either she

wasn't qualified to be president or they didn't know enough about her to have an opinion.

The first four days of her candidacy have brought a series of unwelcome disclosures, personal and political: Her unmarried teenaged daughter's pregnancy, a two-decade-old arrest of her husband on a drunken-driving charge and the hiring of an attorney to represent her in an investigation into the firing of Alaska's public safety commissioner. She has a reputation for attacking wasteful spending, but as mayor of Wasilla, Alaska, she retained a Washington lobbyist to seek $25 million in federal earmarks. She also initially supported $400 million in fed-

eral funding for Alaska's infamous "bridge to nowhere."

When he announced his pick, she and McCain cited her opposition to the bridge project as evidence of her credentials as a reformer.

McCain told reporters Tuesday as he toured a Philadelphia fire station that the vetting process had been "completely thorough."

Even so, some Republicans are nervous.

"I hope that there are no more surprises, that all the homework is done and that she is impressive," says David Frum, a former White House speechwriter for President Bush. "But the fear is, there's a lot of evidence that the homework was not done."

Reinforcing McCain's "brand"

McCain is betting that Palin reinforces his "brand" as a reformer willing to take on established interests, including those in their own party.

Palin was the mayor of Wasilla (population 9,780 in 2007) when she came to statewide attention because of her whistle-blowing on ethics violations by Republican officials. In 2006, she beat Gov. Frank Murkowski in the Republican primary—"a giant-killer," Democratic pollster Celinda Lake recalls—then won the general election.

"People really thought she was a reformer and that was a big plus," says Lake, who was working against her election. "She is a very formidable campaigner, a very formidable debater, very appealing."

Palin, 44 and the mother of five, has en-ergy, poise, a down-to-earth manner and a compelling personal story: from the PTA to the statehouse. She hunts, fishes and rides snowmobiles, pursuits Gingrich says should appeal to blue-collar workers in key states such as Pennsylvania and Ohio.

Her opposition to abortion rights—and her decision to carry to term her now $4^1/_2$-month-old son, Trig, who has Down syndrome—has reassured some evangelicals who have been wary of McCain.

"I have seen a complete turnaround of social conservatives toward the McCain campaign," says Tony Perkins of the Family Research Council.

The campaign also figures Palin's status as the second woman to be on a major party's national ticket could draw female voters, including some who backed Democ-

Charles Gibson talks to Republican Vice Presidential candidate Governor Sarah Palin in her home state of Alaska during an exclusive interview.

rat Hillary Rodham Clinton.

"I am delighted to see the historic nature of this," says Geraldine Ferraro, the former New York congresswoman who in 1984 was the first woman on a national ticket. "Barack Obama's candidacy is history. (Palin's) now is history. One of them is going to get to the door of the White House and pull down a sign that...says, 'Whites only' or 'Men only.' "

But Ferraro doubts that will be enough to draw the votes of many women—including her own. "I'm a Democrat," she says. "I think women, like men, will vote for the top of the ticket."

In USA TODAY polls, McCain's standing among women didn't budge with the pick of Palin. He was backed by 42% of women in a poll taken before the convention, another on the day of her announcement and a third taken Saturday and Sunday.

Ferraro's example also underscores a potential downside of Palin's pick. At the 1984 Democratic convention, her nomination prompted an emotional celebration. Within weeks, she was enmeshed in a controversy over her husband's financial dealings that lasted through Election Day.

Palin has not been a familiar figure on the national stage—or even to McCain.

McCain met her for the first time in February at a National Governors Association meeting, where they chatted privately for perhaps 15 minutes. They met in person for a second time last week, when he invited her to his ranch in Sedona, Ariz. There, McCain offered her a spot on his ticket.

Just how deeply the campaign probed her background and finances isn't clear. The campaign dispatched staffers to Alaska this week, but spokesman Brian Rogers says they aren't investigating Palin. They are there "to coordinate and facilitate communications" with Palin's family and friends.

The scrutiny of a national campaign has sometimes been embarrassing, even disastrous.

For Dan Quayle, picked by the elder George Bush as his running mate in 1988, questions about his service in the National Guard and admission to law school created the impression Quayle was a political lightweight. In 1972, the revelation that Missouri Sen. Thomas Eagleton had undergone shock therapy forced him off the Democratic ticket. That didn't help the beleaguered nominee, George McGovern. He lost 49 states.

"He's catering, or he's folding"

Palin may do more for McCain's base than for the swing voters he needs to attract.

Teresa Ludwig, 56, a health and safety officer at the University of Minnesota, participated in the roundtable with undecided voters Sunday, sponsored by AARP. She voted for Ralph Nader in 2000 and John Kerry in 2004. This year, she attended the state's Democratic caucuses for Clinton but was weighing a vote for McCain because of his maverick image and history of bipartisanship.

Now McCain's choice of Palin has made her lean toward the Democrats again.

"When he picked Palin, I was just, 'Oh, gee, I know who won on this one.' It was just placating to the religious-right base," Ludwig says. "He's catering, or he's folding." The opportunity to elect a woman doesn't sway this former Clinton supporter. "We can't be bought that easy," she says.

"If something does happen to McCain, and she ends up being president, we're in big trouble," says Wendy Brumm, 53, of Ham Lake, who works in an after-school program and joined the roundtable.

Still, Brumm admires Palin's opposition to abortion and finds her intriguing. "She's got potential," Brumm says. "I think she's got a lot of guts."

Palin's biggest test could come Oct. 2 in St. Louis, at the debate between the vice presidential candidates. That will be a prime opportunity to settle questions about her qualifications.

"It's like bringing somebody up from Triple A to the majors during the World Series," says David Keene, president of the American Conservative Union and a Palin supporter. "It's not the same game and nobody knows if they're going to be able to hit the pitches or not."

The McCain campaign's dominant argument against Obama has been that he's not ready to be president. Palin's short resume—she has been governor for less than 20 months—doesn't undercut that, McCain strategist Schmidt says.

"She is, by any objective measurement, more experienced and more accomplished than Sen. Obama," Schmidt says. "She's the governor of a state, she deals with multibillion-dollar budgets, she has a record of accomplishment."

McCain's wife, Cindy, has joined the defense. "Alaska is the closest part of our continent to Russia. So it's not as if she doesn't understand what's at stake here," Cindy McCain said Sunday on ABC's This Week.

Obama's running mate, Delaware Sen. Joe Biden, is everything Palin is not. At 65, he is a six-term senator and chairman of the Senate Foreign Relations Committee, on a first-name basis with foreign leaders worldwide.

But Palin's candidacy and the vice presidential debate presents risks for Biden, too.

She is a matter-of-fact Alaskan; he is a Washington fixture with a reputation for verbosity. In referring to women, he has tended to mention style as well as substance. Last week, he introduced wife Jill as "drop-dead gorgeous" before he mentioned her doctorate in education. On Sunday, he described Palin to an Ohio crowd as "good looking."

In a debate, Biden's self-confidence could come across as condescending or even bullying.

That's a lesson then-congressman Rick Lazio learned when he debated Clinton during the 2000 New York Senate race. He crossed the stage to her lectern, waving a written pledge on campaign finance and urging her to sign it. Some female voters recoiled, and Lazio's poll standing slumped.

"There's no way she was intimidated, but that wasn't the point. I should have been smarter about how the audience was going to view that," Lazio says. "If I was Biden, I'd be thinking about that." ●

AP Images

Democratic Gov. Chris Gregoire, left, and Republican Dino Rossi answer questions during their first debate on September 20, 2008, in Seattle.

Washington

Total population   6,468,424

State population rank   13th

Median household income

Wash.	**$55,591**
USA	**$50,740**

Race/ethnicity (as % of total pop.)

White **84.6%**

5.1% Other

3.6% Black

6.7% Asian

Non-Hispanic **91%**
Hispanic **9%**

11   **Electoral votes**

2004 general election result

✔ Kerry (D) **53%**

   Bush (R) **46%**

2008 primary/caucus winners

✔ Obama (D)

✔ McCain (R)

Note: Each candidate won both the state caucus and primary.

Party strength

	D	R
Governor	✔	
Senators	✔✔	
Representatives	6	3

Deep divide splits Washington state

Voters happy to hop parties as they move down ballot

By William M. Welch • Excerpt from Tuesday, October 28, 2008 • RENTON

If this election is about change, as Barack Obama and John McCain say, Democrats here in Washington state are asking voters not to go too far.

An increasingly blue state on the national electoral map, Washington hasn't voted for a Republican for president since Ronald Reagan in 1984.

Washington is more evenly split politically when it comes to local politics, and a close rematch in the governor's race is proving that once again.

First-term Democratic Gov. Christine Gregoire, 61, who won by 133 votes out of 2.8 million cast, is facing the man she beat in 2004, Republican Dino Rossi, in a tough re-election fight.

"It's hard to be running with a national message of change and still turn around and say, 'We don't want any here,'" says Cathy Allen, a Democratic political consultant in Seattle.

Rossi, a former state senator, has been hitting Gregoire with calls for change in TV ads. Rossi, 49, points out that under Gregoire, the state has seen higher unemployment, an increase in the gasoline tax, rising business failures and a $3.2 billion deficit.

Gregoire has been countering with the difference between the two on social issues. A former state attorney general, she points out in ads that Rossi opposes abortion: "In these tough times, don't turn back the clock. Dino Rossi is not the change we need."

Washington's politics reflect a divide between Seattle, overwhelmingly Democratic and liberal, and the area east of the Cascade Mountains, where Republicans tend to do well and at least one poll shows Rossi besting Gregoire 2-1.

Both presidential and governor's races may be decided in this in-between battleground east of Seattle and Lake Washington. Interviews with voters here showed sharp divisions over the presidential race but also a willingness among many voters to split their tickets.

Luke Esser, state Republican Party chairman, says straight-ticket voting isn't expected in Washington, where voters don't register by party: "In this state, it's every candidate for him or herself," he says. ●

Served six terms in House: Green Party candidate Cynthia McKinney is on the ballot in 31 states—but not her home state of Georgia.

Georgia

Total population 9,544,750

State population rank 9th

Median household income

Ga. **$49,136**
USA **$50,740**

Race/ethnicity (as % of total pop.)

White **65.6%**

1.6% Other **2.8%** Asian **30%** Black

Non-Hispanic **92%**
Hispanic **8%**

15 Electoral votes

2004 general election result

✔ Bush (R) **58%**
Kerry (D) **41%**

2008 primary winners

✔ Obama (D)
✔ Huckabee (R)

Party strength D R

	D	R
Governor		✔
Senators		✔✔
Representatives	6	7

AP Images

Third-party hopefuls hail from Georgia

McKinney unlikely to have major impact on state's Nov. 4 results

By Larry Copeland • Excerpt from Friday, October 3, 2008 • ATLANTA

One is a blunt-spoken former Georgia congressman who helped lead the drive to impeach President Clinton in 1998 and later became a strong advocate of civil liberties after the Sept. 11, 2001, attacks.

The other is a firebrand former Georgia congresswoman who filed articles of impeachment against President Bush and Vice President Cheney and later became an impassioned voice for victims of Hurricane Katrina.

Bob Barr and Cynthia McKinney are two longtime Georgians who are among the best known in a flock of independent candidates running for president this fall as an alternative to Republican candidate John McCain and Democrat Barack Obama.

Barr, 59, the Libertarian Party nominee,

is on the ballot in Georgia and 45 other states and is working to get on in three others. He is running a campaign that rails against the financial policies of both Republicans and Democrats and the growth of the federal government. He opposes the proposed $700 billion rescue package for Wall Street and says the financial industry collapse should be investigated for fraud.

McKinney, 53, Georgia's first African-American congresswoman and the nominee of the Green Party, is on the ballot in 31 states and the District of Columbia—though not in her home state. She advocates an immediate moratorium on home foreclosures and a full pullout of all military forces from Iraq.

Despite Barr's home-state roots, political analysts here say he is unlikely to have a major impact on the race between McCain and Obama for Georgia's 15 electoral votes.

Third-party candidates usually poll better early in a campaign when voters disgruntled by major-party candidates consider voting for them, says Larry Sabato, a political scientist at the University of Virginia. "But as you approach Election Day, it is obvious that either the Democrat or the Republican will be elected president," he says. "At that point, people do not want to throw away their vote." ●

Voting yes: William Adams, 51, fears his church, the Church of Jesus Christ of Latter-day Saints, could be sued for discrimination for not recognizing gay couples.

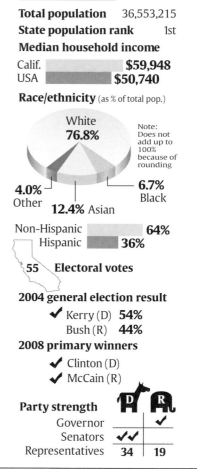

California

Total population   36,553,215

State population rank   1st

Median household income

Calif.   **$59,948**
USA   **$50,740**

Race/ethnicity (as % of total pop.)

White
76.8%

Note: Does not add up to 100% because of rounding

4.0% Other   **12.4%** Asian   **6.7%** Black

Non-Hispanic   **64%**
Hispanic   **36%**

55 Electoral votes

2004 general election result

✔ Kerry (D) **54%**
Bush (R) **44%**

2008 primary winners

✔ Clinton (D)
✔ McCain (R)

Party strength

	D	R
Governor		✔
Senators	✔✔	
Representatives	34	19

Californians go to "war" over proposed gay-marriage ban

For many, Proposition 8 vote as big as presidential race

By William M. Welch • Excerpt from Wednesday, October 29, 2008 • LOS ANGELES

There is little suspense over the presidential race here, but a ballot initiative to overturn gay marriage is garnering the attention of politicians, activists and big spenders.

Proposition 8, which would amend California's constitution to define marriage as between a man and a woman, was put on the ballot after a state Supreme Court ruling in May said a ban on gay marriage was unconstitutional.

The ruling triggered a rush to the altar by gay and lesbian couples, including many from other states seeking legal recognition of their unions. That prompted what has become a pricey and exuberant battle.

"This is the most expensive cultural war in America, ever," says John Duran, a West Hollywood City Council member and fundraiser for opponents of Prop 8. "It's a cultural war over the role of gay and lesbian Americans in California."

Opponents of same-sex marriages are determined to trump the court at the ballot box and have unleashed a massive campaign of organizing, television ads and fundraising.

Their early success at fundraising forced gay-marriage advocates to step up their own campaign efforts, and now the two sides are on track to spend more than $60 million, about evenly divided. The issue has made impromptu demonstrations a common sight across Southern California, as people from both sides wave signs at motorists from suburban street corners.

California's record as a trend-setter for the rest of the nation means the implications go beyond the borders of a state that is home to roughly 10% of the nation. While similar issues face voters in Florida and Arizona, both sides believe victory here is of paramount importance to shape public attitudes about same-sex marriage nationally under the next administration.

"This is the second-biggest race in the country," says Sonja Eddings Brown, spokeswoman for the Yes on 8 campaign. "And the impact of Proposition 8 is going to set a precedence for the United States of America."

Geoff Kors, a member of the executive committee of the No on 8 campaign, said, "Every poll suggests this is a dead heat." ●

Always a first time: Mark Jones, 62, of Washington, Ind., says he has never voted for a Democrat for president. This time, the retired teacher says he's leaning toward Barack Obama over John McCain.

Indiana

Total population   6,345,289

State population rank   15th

Median household income

Ind.   **$47,448**
USA   **$50,740**

Race/ethnicity (as % of total pop.)

White
88.1%

1.5% Other   **1.4%** Asian   **9.0%** Black

Non-Hispanic   **95%**
Hispanic   **5%**

11 Electoral votes

2004 general election result
✔ Bush (R)   **60%**
Kerry (D)   **39%**

2008 primary winners
✔ Clinton (D)
✔ McCain (R)

Party strength	D	R
Governor		✔
Senators	✔	✔
Representatives	5	4

Key to taking Indiana rests in capturing southern part

Hoosier state a crossroads for loyalty and leeriness

By Tim Evans and Mary Beth Schneider • Excerpt from Friday, October 31, 2008 • INDIANAPOLIS

The road to winning Indiana's 11 electoral votes—and, potentially, the White House—may go through Mark Jones' living room in southern Indiana.

Jones, a retired 62-year-old teacher from Washington in Daviess County, says he has never voted for a Democrat for president. But in the face of a tough economy and a lingering war, he says he fears Republican John McCain would be a repeat of President Bush.

"I'm probably leaning more toward (Barack) Obama right now," Jones says, "but that still could change."

Middle-class undecided voters such as Jones are essential to the hopes of both Obama and McCain in Indiana.

No Democrat presidential candidate has carried Indiana since Lyndon Johnson in 1964—and no Democrat has won statewide without also doing well in southern Indiana. "I think it's vital," Robert Dion, a political science professor at the University of Evansville, says of southern Indiana's significance this year.

According to Jonathan Swain, communications director for the Obama campaign in Indiana, Obama has made 47 campaign stops in the state.

McCain has made six campaign stops, according to Jennifer Hallowell, the former executive director of the Indiana Republican Party.

Ron Sharp, 55, a loan officer from Petersburg in Pike County who voted twice for Bill Clinton and twice for Bush, says he wants to see the United States drill for oil in more places. "I'm having a real hard time with liberal Democrat tree-huggers not wanting to drill up there on a little spit of land in Alaska," Sharp says.

But, Sharp also says he believes the Iraq war is "a waste of time" and money—a view he shares with Obama.

Sharp says he is leaning toward McCain, primarily because of the Arizona senator's experience and his concern that Obama is too liberal. He also likes Palin's conservative stance on social issues.

Jones, the retired teacher, says he is concerned about the economy and sees McCain's approach as "the same old Bush" tactics. ●

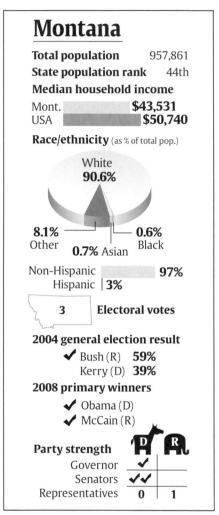

Wind and coal: Peter Wipf is a member of a Hutterite colony that has leased land to a wind energy company.

Montana

Total population	957,861
State population rank	44th

Median household income

Mont.	**$43,531**
USA	**$50,740**

Race/ethnicity (as % of total pop.)

White **90.6%**

8.1% Other

0.7% Asian

0.6% Black

Non-Hispanic **97%**
Hispanic **3%**

3 Electoral votes

2004 general election result
- ✔ Bush (R) **59%**
- Kerry (D) **39%**

2008 primary winners
- ✔ Obama (D)
- ✔ McCain (R)

Party strength

	D	R
Governor	✔	
Senators	✔✔	
Representatives	0	1

Montana sharply split over candidates' energy policies

Focus is on fossil fuels versus alternative energy sources

By Karl Puckett • Excerpt from Friday, October 31, 2008 • GREAT FALLS

Wind farm development has many Montanans turning green. Now the question is how many of them will turn blue when they vote for president Tuesday.

Since 2006, 178 giant turbines have sprouted in farm fields at four commercial facilities churning out a combined 270 megawatts of electricity, with even more projects in the planting stages, according to the state Department of Commerce.

Energy policy is front and center for presidential candidates John McCain and Barack Obama, and Montana, where wind and coal are equally abundant, is paying close attention.

"They are all promising alternative energy," says Peter Wipf, who says he tends to vote Republican but remains undecided.

Obama's policies supporting renewable energy are striking a chord with many Montanans who are boosting energy produced from wind, solar and biofuels, says Theresa Keaveny, executive director of Montana Conservation Voters in Billings. McCain, she adds, has consistently opposed alternative energy and supports more oil drilling, "which Montanans don't want."

Montana has 120 billion tons of coal reserves, the most in the nation, and each year 41 million tons is shipped by train to coal-fired generating plants around the country, according to the Montana Coal Council. McCain's "all of the above" approach, which includes using coal, oil, nuclear and alternative energy, appeals more to Montanans, says Erik Iverson, the chairman of the Montana Republican Party.

"The bottom line is, who are you going to trust to get that coal out of the ground and create jobs?" Iverson says.

Democratic Gov. Brian Schweitzer, who touted the state's "clean and green" energy agenda and Obama in a speech at the August Democratic National Convention in Denver, is running for re-election and is leading Republican challenger Roy Brown 60% to 27%, according to the latest Montana State-Billings poll.

Now Obama is trying to shift the state's political winds for president. He's visited five times—McCain has yet to campaign here.

"It's interesting Obama hasn't given up," says Craig Wilson, a political scientist at Montana State University-Billings. He's predicting a close finish. ●

House calls: Mexican-born Luz Padilla Velasquez, a union activist and new U.S. citizen, does legwork in Las Vegas for Barack Obama.

Nevada

Total population   2,565,382

State population rank   35th

Median household income

Nev.   **$55,062**
USA   **$50,740**

Race/ethnicity (as % of total pop.)

White
81.4%

4.5%
Other   **6.1%** Asian   **8.0%**
Black

Non-Hispanic   **75%**
Hispanic   **25%**

5   Electoral votes

2004 general election result

✓ Bush (R)   **50%**
Kerry (D)   **48%**

2008 caucus winners

✓ Clinton (D)[1]
✓ Romney (R)

1 – Clinton won more votes, Obama more delegates.

Party strength

	D	R
Governor		✓
Senators	✓	✓
Representatives	1	2

Working on winning union vote in Nevada

Traditional GOP state in play because of labor, Latino forces

By Anjeanette Damon • Excerpt from Thursday, October 30, 2008 • LAS VEGAS

Luz Padilla Velasquez may not look like your typical union shop steward. The 26-year-old mother of three, a Mexican immigrant who recently became a U.S. citizen, doesn't work in a factory or a mill or a manufacturing plant. She's a housekeeper in a hotel-casino on the Las Vegas Strip.

She's also on the front line of an army of union reps working member by member to turn out voters throughout Nevada, a battleground state in the race for the White House and a vanguard in the new generation of the nation's labor movement.

For Democratic presidential nominee Barack Obama, labor unions in Nevada have become a formidable turnout force targeting some of the constituencies most important to his campaign: Latino voters and women.

Velasquez is one of hundreds of paid union canvassers working to identify, influence and turn out more than 100,000 voters.

In Nevada, where presidential elections traditionally are very close, that organization could mean the difference between victory and defeat.

"It could be a very positive factor for Obama," says Eric Herzik, a political scientist at the University of Nevada-Reno. "When labor gets motivated, they are an important force."

Unlike traditional manufacturing-based economies, Nevada's service-based industry has proved fertile ground for union organizers.

As a result, more than 15% of the workforce is represented by unions, according to statistics from the U.S. Department of Labor.

More important for Obama, union households accounted for 26% of the vote in the 2006 statewide election, according to exit polls.

Also, unlike traditional union-dense states such as Michigan or Pennsylvania, the demographics of Nevada's union membership are largely Latino and female, says David MacPherson, an economics professor at Florida State University who tracks labor statistics.

Velasquez, who will be voting for the first time since earning her citizenship, says she was won over by Obama's life story.

"He was raised by a single mom and his grandparents," she says. "I come from a mom like that. My mom raised us, seven of us, and she was the only one working. ●

This home in Pembroke Pines was offered for sale after going into foreclosure. A surplus of homes and condos built during an unprecedented housing boom has left the market saturated and sluggish.

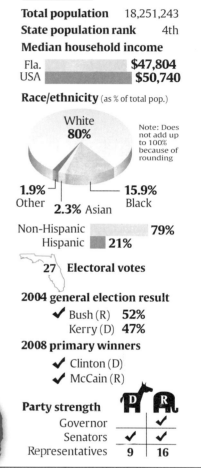

Florida

Total population 18,251,243
State population rank 4th
Median household income

Fla.	**$47,804**
USA	**$50,740**

Race/ethnicity (as % of total pop.)

White **80%**

Note: Does not add up to 100% because of rounding

1.9% Other
2.3% Asian
15.9% Black

Non-Hispanic	**79%**
Hispanic	**21%**

27 **Electoral votes**

2004 general election result
✔ Bush (R) **52%**
Kerry (D) **47%**

2008 primary winners
✔ Clinton (D)
✔ McCain (R)

Party strength	**D**	**R**
Governor		✔
Senators	✔	✔
Representatives	9	16

Fla. has long been feeling housing pains

Mortgage payments, foreclosure filings rise

By Laura Ruane and Rick Neale • Excerpt from Thursday, October 2, 2008 • CAPE CORAL

Long before the debate over a federal bailout of the nation's financial institutions took center stage, sagging property values and soaring mortgage payments triggered in part by adjustable interest rates and increasing taxes threatened to force thousands of Floridians into foreclosure.

According to RealtyTrac, Florida's 44,000 foreclosure filings in August trailed only California's in the number of properties affected. California had 101,724 filings. Florida's foreclosure troubles surpassed the rest of the top five states: Arizona, 14,333; Michigan,13,605; and Nevada, 11,706.

Much like Southern California, Arizona and Nevada, Florida experienced a home-building boom earlier this decade, says David Denslow, professor and research economist at the University of Florida.

"There were lots and lots of people who were busily selling real estate. The home-ownership rate here goes up from 66% to 72% between 2000 and 2006—that's a huge change," Denslow says.

"All of a sudden, the population growth slowed. The housing sales slowed. And the construction workers left," Denslow says. "And so, we've been in a recession since roughly May of 2007."

McCain has called for the creation of a U.S. Justice Department "mortgage abuse task force." It would "offer assistance to state attorney generals who are investigating abusive lending practices," says Mario Diaz, McCain's Southeast regional communication director.

Obama has said he wants to create a "universal mortgage credit" for about 10 million homeowners, most of whom earn less than $50,000 per year. The average credit would be $500, he has said.

Cindy Kelley, president of the Merritt Island-based Space Coast Association of Realtors, says she doubts either Obama or McCain can fix Florida's real estate mess.

"The bottom line is, the president doesn't have that kind of power," she says. ●

A name tag that says "I speak Arabic" in Arabic is seen on Mohamad Atwi, Wal-Mart's store manager in Dearborn. An aisle of this new Wal-Mart features many items geared toward Arab Americans.

Michigan

Total population 10,071,822

State population rank 8th

Median household income

Mich. **$47,950**

USA **$50,740**

Race/ethnicity (as % of total pop.)

White **81.2%**

Note: Does not add up to 100% because of rounding

2.2% Other

2.4% Asian

14.3% Black

Non-Hispanic **96%**

Hispanic **4%**

17 Electoral votes

2004 general election result

✔ Kerry (D) **51%**

Bush (R) **48%**

2008 primary winners

✔ Clinton (D)

✔ Romney (R)

Party strength

	D	R
Governor	✔	
Senators	✔	✔
Representatives	6	9

Arab Americans hold sway in Mich.

In Dearborn, their views on jobs, war give Obama an edge

By Kathleen Gray • Excerpt from Wednesday, October 8, 2008 • DEARBORN

A li Dagher and Belal Abdallah came here as kids, brought by parents looking for the opportunities that abounded in the boom years of the 1970s.

Dagher and Abdallah, Muslims whose families are from Lebanon, became fast friends here in the city with the nation's largest concentration of Arab Americans.

They achieved success beyond their dreams, Dagher as a lawyer and Abdallah as a doctor of internal medicine. Now they are the only two among their immigrant friends left in Michigan.

"We came here for two reasons—economic opportunity and liberty—and now we have neither," says Dagher, 42. He talks about the poor economy and sees erosion of Arab Americans' civil liberties since 9/11. "Everybody else has left because there are more opportunities overseas."

Both men say they will vote for Democrat Barack Obama for president.

Arab Americans overwhelmingly cite the economy and the continuing loss of jobs as reasons they want to see a change in Washington and Obama leading that change. In addition, a deep dismay with the policies of President Bush, particularly on the Middle East and the war in Iraq, is leading them to turn away from Republican John McCain and his support for the Iraq war.

In a national poll last month by the Arab American Institute, a poll of 500 Arab Americans gave Obama a 54%-33% lead over McCain. Throw in the Independent and Green Party candidates and Obama's lead slips to 46%-32%.

"There is more enthusiasm at the grass-roots level for him," says James Zogby, president of the institute.

Michigan is home to the second-largest population of Arab Americans in the nation, after California. In 2007, the Census estimated 1.5 million people of Arab ancestry in the country, 157,000 of them in Michigan. In Dearborn, 30% of residents are Arab American.

Unemployment, fed by automakers' downsizing and plant closings, is 8.9%, the highest rate in the nation. Obama's campaign theme of "change" is resonating. ●

Black voter turnout traditionally high: Lafeyounda Brooks, president of the Jackson State University NAACP student chapter, greets attendees at Democratic Convention Watch Party on campus.

Mississippi

Total population   2,918,785

State population rank   31st

Median household income

Miss.   **$36,338**
USA   **$50,740**

Race/ethnicity (as % of total pop.)

White **60.7%**

1.3% Other

0.8% Asian

37.2% Black

Non-Hispanic **98%**
Hispanic **2%**

6   **Electoral votes**

2004 general election result
✔ Bush (R)   **59%**
Kerry (D)   **40%**

2008 primary winners
✔ Obama (D)
✔ McCain (R)

Party strength   D   R
Governor   ✔
Senators   ✔✔
Representatives   3   1

History on GOP side in Miss. presidential vote

Dems target large voter turnout to reverse traditional election results

By Chris Joyner • Excerpt from Friday, September 26, 2008 • JACKSON

It was like something out of a movie about Mississippi, the kind of scene that frames the state in historical terms of race and politics.

About 100 students and some faculty members had gathered in the student center at Jackson State University, a historically black university, to watch Sen. Barack Obama accept the Democratic nomination for president on television.

During one of the night's down moments, local Democratic organizers lowered the sound on the sets and held a question-and-answer session. The crowd quieted as 9-year-old Taylor Carr, son of the university women's basketball coach Denise Taylor, took the microphone.

"I want to know if Barack Obama will be in my history book next year," he said.

A number of people in the audience assured Taylor that, yes, Obama would be in his history books. But if he does become the nation's first African American elected to the presidency in November, it's not likely Mississippi will be the reason.

While an American Research Group poll conducted in Mississippi in mid-September showed Obama with 88% of likely black voters in his camp, the same poll showed Republican nominee John McCain with 55% of the overall vote and 85% of the white vote.

U.S. Census data show that African Americans in Mississippi take the right to vote seriously. One in three Mississippians

are black, the largest percentage of any state, and they vote in large numbers. Only three states—Illinois, Kentucky and Missouri—had a higher black turnout in that election, Census figures show.

Keia Johnson, a 20-year-old political science major at Jackson State, said the importance of Obama's candidacy is not lost on her. "It's not just a place where we live," Johnson said. "It's a place where we can change things, make things happen."

Even though Jacobs believes McCain will carry the state, she thinks a lot of voters in north Mississippi are enthusiastic about Obama. "I think he will do very well," she said. "But it's the white vote he needs." ●

Steelworkers, from left, Charles Johnstone, Mark Plant, Brian Ulrich, Craig Plant and Bob Ulrich, stand outside the Amweld plant in Niles, Ohio, where they once worked.

Ohio

Total population 11,466,917

State population rank 7th

Median household income

Ohio	$46,597
USA	$50,740

Race/ethnicity (as % of total pop.)

White **84.9%**

1.6% Other

1.6% Asian

12% Black

Non-Hispanic	**98%**
Hispanic	**2%**

20 Electoral votes

2004 general election result

✔ Bush (R) **51%**
Kerry (D) **49%**

2008 primary winners

✔ Clinton (D)
✔ McCain (R)

Party strength

	D	R
Governor	✔	
Senators	✔	✔
Representatives	7	11

Manufacturing losses weigh heavily on Ohio

Trade dominates political rhetoric as state struggles to replace jobs

By David J. Lynch • Excerpt from Monday, March 3, 2008 • NILES

It's late morning on a workday, a time when these men would normally be found on the factory floor. Now they sit around a table in a one-story steelworkers union office and wonder what they'll do with the rest of their working lives.

After more than 60 years in business, their employer, Amweld Building Products, announced in October that it was closing two local plants and shipping the work to Monterrey, Mexico. Amweld blamed rising costs for energy, health care and workers' compensation for the elimination of jobs paying an average of $18 per hour.

Ohio's Mahoning Valley once was emblematic of industrial America, thickly populated with auto and steel plants, employing men whose strong backs and high school diplomas were their chief credentials.

In December, the U.S. Labor Department certified the steelworkers' lost jobs as trade-related, making the men eligible for aid under the federal Trade Adjustment Assistance (TAA) program. "A significant number of workers at the firm are age 50 or over and possess skills that are not easily transferable. Competitive conditions within the industry are adverse," read the government's antiseptic conclusion. The workers get two years of help with health care coverage, relocation allowances and retraining.

But as safety nets go, this is a thin one, and individual circumstances of age and health shape their decisions. At 32 years old, Brian Ulrich feels he's young enough to start over, so the former high school football player has gone back to school, studying nursing at Kent State. When he graduates in two years, he figures he'll be able to earn almost $50,000 annually, about what he made at Amweld.

His dad, Bob, who started at Amweld after a tour of duty in Vietnam, has made a different choice. For him, times were good as recently as two years ago when he made a career-best $54,000. Learning a new career at age 58 doesn't seem like such a good idea. "If I go to school for two years, I'd be a 60-year-old man looking for work. It'd be ludicrous," he says. ●

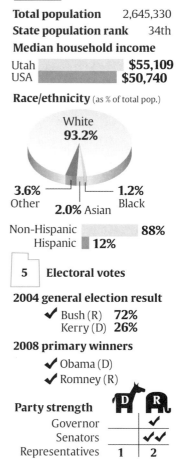

Ashlee Dent, left, and Kimmie Goodson register to vote at the Downtown Farmers' Market in Salt Lake City on Sept. 6. The state has more than four times as many registered Republicans as Democrats.

Utah

Total population	2,645,330
State population rank	34th

Median household income

Utah	**$55,109**
USA	**$50,740**

Race/ethnicity (as % of total pop.)

White
93.2%

3.6% Other   **2.0%** Asian   **1.2%** Black

Non-Hispanic	**88%**
Hispanic	**12%**

5 Electoral votes

2004 general election result

✔ Bush (R) **72%**
  Kerry (D) **26%**

2008 primary winners

✔ Obama (D)
✔ Romney (R)

Party strength	**D**	**R**
Governor		✔
Senators		✔✔
Representatives	1	2

Conservative bent of Utah favors GOP

Last Democrat to win state was Johnson in '64

By **Brian Passey** • Excerpt from Monday, September 22, 2008 • ST. GEORGE

There aren't many states on a political map redder than Utah. Utah voters have not given a majority of their votes to a Democratic candidate since President Lyndon Johnson's landslide victory over Sen. Barry Goldwater in 1964.

That's unlikely to change this year. According to a statewide poll by Dan Jones & Associates, conducted Sept. 8-11, Republican presidential nominee John McCain leads Democratic nominee Barack Obama 62%-24% among registered voters.

Obama supporters in Utah understand their candidate has almost no chance of winning the state's five electoral votes. Even so, Democrats say they do not expect McCain to retain Bush's high marks from four years ago.

"I personally think that Utahans have much more in common with Sen. Obama than they do with Sen. McCain in terms of values," says James McMahon of Brookside, an independent who says he gravitated toward Obama early.

Utah Democrats know that recruiting supporters means starting small and often staying there.

Just a handful of people attended the first meeting to organize southern Utah supporters at a local coffee shop May 28, McMahon says. A few weeks later, a barbecue in a St. George park drew about 100, he says. Nevertheless, volunteers such as Lindsey Witt of St. George remain determined.

"I'm voting for someone I think can really make a difference," Witt says. "Even though my vote may not be counted, I think it will be heard."

Utah is a state where conservative politics are often linked to its deeply religious population, a majority of whom are members of the Church of Jesus Christ of Latter-day Saints. Jeff Eastwood, 51, of Toquerville, a member of the LDS Church who supports McCain, says, "We generally tend to follow people that have more conservative values."

Witt grew up believing the Republican Party best fit her moral and religious beliefs. Then, she says, she saw Obama on Oprah. Witt began to study his platform and decided it aligned more precisely with her values.

"Contrary to popular belief, not all Mormons have to be Republicans," she says. ●

Firm believer: Laura Wells and her husband, Cedric, both supporters of Republican John McCain, say they're hoping for a McCain presidency—not a victory in the liberal-leaning state.

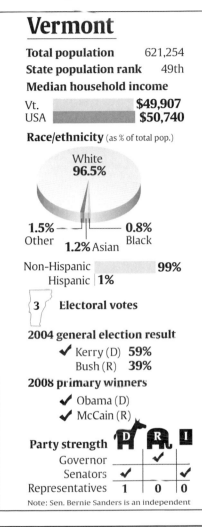

Vermont

Total population	621,254
State population rank	49th

Median household income

Vt.	**$49,907**
USA	**$50,740**

Race/ethnicity (as % of total pop.)

White
96.5%

1.5% — Other
0.8% Black
1.2% Asian

Non-Hispanic **99%**
Hispanic **1%**

3 **Electoral votes**

2004 general election result
- ✔ Kerry (D) **59%**
- Bush (R) **39%**

2008 primary winners
- ✔ Obama (D)
- ✔ McCain (R)

Party strength

	D	R	I
Governor		✔	
Senators	✔		✔
Representatives	1	0	0

Note: Sen. Bernie Sanders is an independent

Republicans a rare find in blue Vermont

"Uphill battle" waged in Green Mountain State

By Adam Silverman • Excerpt from Monday, October 6, 2008 • UNDERHILL CENTER

Something looks out of place in front of the Wells Corner Market here in left-leaning Underhill Center, a hamlet in a liberal county in a dark-blue state.

There are yard signs cheering John McCain's candidacy for president.

A traveler driving the three miles from the nearest state highway into town along River Road will pass many more placards for Barack Obama.

For store proprietors Cedric and Laura Wells, that's no matter. Their support for McCain has nothing to do with his chances here.

"You've got to voice your opinion no matter what," says Cedric, 53. "It's not depressing." Laura, 50, says, "We live in a liberal town, but we love our neighbors. They're good people. We discuss politics and religion—all the stuff you're not supposed to."

Vermont Republicans and McCain campaign organizers are glad contested New Hampshire is right next-door. McCain volunteers are driving over the Connecticut River and into the Granite State to work toward winning there, says McCain's New England regional campaign manager, Jim Barnett, a former chairman of the Vermont Republican Party.

"It's tough doing business there," Barnett says of supporters in the Green Mountain State, "but they're also positioned well to help us in a key swing state across the river. There are a limited number of states around this country that are going to swing this election. When it comes time to allocate scarce resources, we have a critical battleground across the river in New Hampshire."

The Obama campaign, comfortably ahead, is not taking Vermont for granted. Paid staffers are working out of two campaign offices, phone banks and even a recent "Camp Obama" that trained volunteers to be field organizers in battleground states, says Gannet Tseggai, a Northeast regional Obama spokeswoman.

"We are certainly committed to Vermont," she says. "We have a great group of supporters and enthusiastic volunteers. We value every single vote. We're going to fight for every single vote between now and Election Day." ●

In St. Louis: Democratic presidential candidate Barack Obama drew nearly 100,000 people to a rally Oct. 18 under the Gateway Arch.

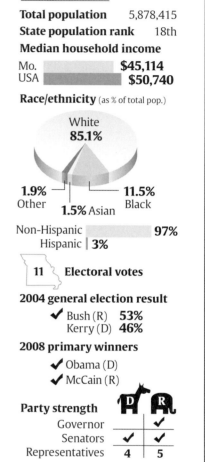

Missouri

Total population	5,878,415
State population rank	18th

Median household income

Mo.	**$45,114**
USA	**$50,740**

Race/ethnicity (as % of total pop.)

White **85.1%**

1.9% Other
1.5% Asian
11.5% Black

Non-Hispanic **97%**
Hispanic **3%**

11 **Electoral votes**

2004 general election result

✔ Bush (R) **53%**
Kerry (D) **46%**

2008 primary winners

✔ Obama (D)
✔ McCain (R)

Party strength

	D	R
Governor		✔
Senators	✔	✔
Representatives	4	5

Missouri has gift for picking presidents

Close race could test hot streak

By Dirk Vanderhart • Excerpt from Monday, November 3, 2008 • SPRINGFIELD

It's been 52 years since Missouri, the nation's most consistent bellwether state, failed to correctly pick the winner of a presidential contest.

Recent polls show the state in a dead heat, even though Democratic presidential nominee Sen. Barack Obama consistently leads in national polls.

The most recent state poll by American Research Group, conducted Oct. 28-30, showed the race in a tie, with Republican candidate Sen. John McCain and Obama each getting 48%.

"The Democrats forget that this country isn't just East and West coasts, and a few big cities in between," said Kevin Smith, 42, who was among thousands in attendance to see Republican vice presidential candidate Sarah Palin speak at a Springfield rally in late October. "There's a whole lot of towns just like Springfield, too."

Democratic strength in the state has long resided in the urban centers of St. Louis and Kansas City, as well as liberal bastions such as Columbia, said George Connor, a professor of political science at Missouri State University in Springfield.

"Missouri is still a conservative state at its heart," Connor said.

There is evidence the Illinois senator could inspire enough turnout in urban areas to offset the Republican advantage elsewhere, Connor said.

He pointed to an Oct. 18 rally under St. Louis' Gateway Arch at which Obama drew an estimated 100,000 spectators.

The Republican ticket has seen high interest as well. An estimated 15,000 attended an Oct. 24 rally with Palin in Springfield, the state's third-largest city.

Many at the rally cited Palin's morals and down-to-earth parlance as reasons for supporting her.

"We're worried about America," said 48-year-old Amber Theobald, a Republican. "We just wish America would stop drinking Obama juice."

David Robertson, a political science professor at the University of Missouri-St. Louis, predicted Obama has a 55% chance of taking Missouri, compared to a 75% chance of winning the election.

"We're usually within 3% or less of the popular vote nationwide," Robertson said. "If that's the case, then I think we go with Obama." ●

Back-and-forth: Ed Brown joins the political discourse at Carino Coffee in Aurora, Colo. "One day I say, 'Yep, I'm for Obama, and the next day I say, 'Nope, I'm for McCain,'" he said, before settling on his choice.

Colorado

Total population   4,861,515

State population rank   22nd

Median household income

Colo.	**$52,212**
USA	**$50,740**

Race/ethnicity (as % of total pop.)

White
89.9%

3.2% Other   **2.7%** Asian   **4.2%** Black

Non-Hispanic	**80%**
Hispanic	**20%**

9   **Electoral votes**

2004 general election result

✔ Bush (R)   **52%**
  Kerry (D)   **47%**

2008 caucus winners

✔ Obama (D)
✔ Romney (R)

Party strength   **D**   **R**

	D	R
Governor	✔	
Senators	✔	✔
Representatives	4	3

Changes in suburbia make Colorado a new bellwether

Election to test inroads by Dems

By Susan Page • Excerpt from Monday, November 3, 2008 • AURORA

The bustling Carino Coffee shop in this Denver suburb just might be the new center of the political universe.

Locals drop by for a cup of coffee and a rolling political debate before heading off to errands or jobs at the engineering and tech firms that have sprung up in the area. All five people lingering around one table on this particular morning are registered as Republicans or independents, but only two plan to vote for John McCain for president. Two are supporting Barack Obama. One is flummoxed.

"One day I say, 'Yep, I'm for Obama, and the next day I say, 'Nope, I'm for McCain,'" says Ed Brown, 64, retired from the Air Force and Defense Department. On his mail-in ballot, he has marked a choice in every contest except the one at the top.

The influx and shifting allegiances of college-educated voters in suburbs like this one have helped turn Colorado from a reliably Republican state to one that some political analysts consider the nation's new bellwether. Similar demographic trends in Northern Virginia and along the Interstate 4 corridor in central Florida have boosted Democratic prospects in those traditionally red states, too.

This is the political legacy of the 2008 election: fundamental changes in the electoral map and the parties, including which states and what voters are up for grabs. The emergence of the Mountain West as a battleground and Democratic inroads among suburban voters across the country are changes likely to reverberate well beyond the McCain vs. Obama contest Tuesday.

For one thing, Colorado seems poised to replace Missouri as the nation's leading bellwether — the state most likely to reflect the nation's leanings. "I said in December '06 that if you tell me (who wins) Colorado, I will know who wins the White House in 2008," says veteran political analyst Bernadette Budde of BIPAC, the Business Industry Political Action Committee.

Says Gov. Bill Ritter: "The independent voter can no longer be counted on as reliably for Republicans," in part because Democrats are nominating different sorts of candidates. ●

Decision is in voters' hands

U.S. history will be made today by electing McCain or Obama

By William M. Welch • Excerpt from Tuesday, November 4, 2008

Last-second appeal: Sarah Palin speaks to supporters in Dubuque, Iowa, on November 3.

Americans go to the polls today to make a historic selection, either the first African American president or the oldest first-term occupant of the White House and his female vice president.

Republican John McCain and his running mate, Sarah Palin, made frenetic final dashes across several crucial states where the winner could be decided, working for a poll-defying upset. Democrat Barack Obama, ahead in many national polls, kept a more leisurely campaign pace.

"My attitude is, if we've done everything we can do, then it's up to the people to decide," Obama told a radio interviewer.

McCain sounded more like the underdog. "Don't give up hope. Be strong," he told crowds. "Nothing is inevitable here."

Obama announced the death of his grandmother, Madelyn Dunham, after her battle with cancer. He had interrupted campaigning last month to visit her. In a statement with his sister, Obama said, "She was the cornerstone of our family, and a woman of extraordinary accomplishment, strength and humility."

Besides deciding control of the White House, voters in 33 states were electing 35 U.S. senators, as Democrats bid to build on their fragile 51-49 voting majority. Much of the fight was on GOP turf — 23 of the seats at stake are held by Republicans, and five of those have no incumbent running; 12 are held by Democrats.

All 435 seats in the U.S. House of Representatives are up. Democrats were confident of increasing their 235-199 majority.

Eleven states are selecting governors, with particularly tight races in North Carolina and Washington for seats now held by Democrats. Republicans were hoping to trim the Democrats' 28-22 edge in governors.

Voters were deciding 153 ballot measures in 36 states. Among them: a ban on same-sex marriage in California and a ban on

most abortions in South Dakota.

Warned of record turnout — perhaps as many as 135 million voters — many people took advantage of state laws that permit early voting. More than 29 million Americans cast early ballots, according to the U.S. Elections Project at George Mason University.

The top concern among elections officials is a heavy turnout overwhelming some polling places — particularly in states without provisions for in-person early voting, such as Pennsylvania.

In North Carolina, where Obama was hoping to become the first Democratic nominee to carry the state since 1976,

High turnout: More than 63 million Americans cast their ballot for Barack Obama.

2.6 million early ballots were cast. In Ohio, a battleground McCain was fighting to hold, 1.5 million early ballots were cast, more than twice as many as in 2004. ●

Obama tells supporters: "This is your victory"

Calls on Americans to rise above partisan pettiness

By Kathy Kiely • Excerpts from Wednesday, November 5, 2008 • CHICAGO

(above) President-elect Barack Obama salutes the crowd at Grant Park in Chicago after being announced as the winner of the 2008 presidential election. (opposite) John McCain delivers remarks during his concession speech in Phoenix, Arizona, on November 4, 2008.

Barack Obama, who introduced himself to the nation four years ago as "a skinny kid with a funny name," celebrated his election Tuesday night as the first African American president before a multiracial crowd of nearly a quarter-million on the shore of Lake Michigan.

"It belongs to you," Obama said from a stage decorated with 25 American flags. "This is your victory."

For Obama, a first-term senator with family connections that span the globe from Kenya to Kansas, it was the dizzying conclusion to an unlikely odyssey.

"I was never the likeliest candidate," he said here.

Moments before he spoke, Obama received congratulatory phone calls from John McCain, the Republican senator he beat, and President Bush.

Robert Gibbs, Obama's spokesman, said the Democratic president-elect thanked McCain for his "graciousness" and a campaign conducted with "class and honor." "I need your help," Obama told McCain. "You're a leader on so many important issues."

Bush invited Obama and his family to visit the White House soon and promised to smooth the transition, White House spokeswoman Dana Perino said.

"You are about to go on one of the great journeys of life," the president told his soon-to-be successor. "Congratulations and go enjoy yourself."

A virtually unknown state legislator when he spoke to the Democratic National Convention in 2004, Obama galvanized viewers by turning his own struggle to come to grips with his biracial identity as the son of an African exchange student and a white American into a metaphor for the nation's need to transcend its own divisions. He echoed that theme in his speech, calling on Americans to rise above "the partisan pettiness and immaturity that has poisoned our politics."

Obama acknowledged the country's struggle with wars in Iraq and Afghanistan, and the worst financial crisis since the Great Depression.

"The road ahead will be long. Our climb will be steep. We may not get there in one year or even one term," Obama said.

He urged Americans to "summon a new spirit of patriotism, of service and responsibility where each of us resolves to pitch in and work harder and look after not only ourselves, but each other."

He said he will fulfill one campaign promise immediately. He told his daughters Malia, 10, and Sasha, 7, that they "have earned the new puppy that's coming with us to the White House."

Obama and running mate Joe Biden continued stumping for votes even as supporters were streaming to the elaborate tent city where they would celebrate with the glittering skyline of Chicago before them.

Obama began his day by casting his ballot at Beulah Shoesmith Elementary School in this city's Hyde Park neighborhood. Then the Democratic presidential nominee took off for one last trip in a campaign plane that has logged 76,820 miles since its inaugural flight, emblazoned with his campaign logo, in July.

Arriving at the United Auto Workers Local 550 union hall in Indianapolis, Obama joined the phone bank, borrowing volunteers' cellphones to participate in the get-out-the-vote work.

"Michael, this is Barack. How are you?" he said to one voter. "I'd like to get your vote. Don't be discouraged if there are some long lines."

Biden voted in his home state of Delaware, then stopped in another Republican stronghold. The veteran Delaware senator greeted voters outside Montrose Elementary School in Richmond, Va.

Later, in Chicago, Biden continued campaigning by satellite all afternoon, doing 27 news interviews in key states.

Obama spent two hours playing basketball in a west Chicago gym with a group of friends including Democratic Sen. Robert Casey of Pennsylvania, then dined at home with his wife, Michelle, and daughters.

Obama held his victory celebration in Grant Park, infamous for the tear-gassing and beating of protesters during the 1968 Democratic National Convention. Now Obama's supporters hope it will be remembered for a different piece of history.

"It makes me feel incredibly good about how far this country has come," Joan Patsios, a Chicago public defender, said as she waited for Obama's arrival. ●

Obama's win means "America is a place where all things are possible"

Excerpts from Barack Obama's victory speech on Tuesday, November 4, 2008

(above) Barack Obama addresses the crowd, and indeed the world, during his victory speech at Grant Park in Chicago. (opposite) Obama and his family, including wife Michelle and daughters Sasha and Malia Ann, celebrate Obama's remarkable victory.

"**I**f there is anyone out there who still doubts that America is a place where all things are possible, who still wonders if the dream of our founders is alive in our time, who still questions the power of our democracy, tonight is your answer.

"While she's no longer with us, I know my grandmother's watching, along with the family that made me who I am. I miss them tonight. I know that my debt to them is beyond measure.

"I will never forget who this victory truly belongs to. It belongs to you. ... We didn't start with much money or many endorsements. Our campaign was not hatched in the halls of Washington. ... It was built by working men and women who dug into what little savings they had to give $5 and $10 and $20 to the cause.

"There's new energy to harness, new jobs to be created, new schools to build, and threats to meet, alliances to repair.

"The road ahead will be long. Our climb will be steep. We may not get there in one year or even in one term. But, America, I have never been more hopeful than I am tonight that we will get there. I promise you, we as a people will get there.

"That's the true genius of America: that America can change. Our union can be perfected. What we've already achieved gives us hope for what we can and must achieve tomorrow.

"This election had many firsts and many stories that will be told for generations. But one that's on my mind tonight's about a woman who cast her ballot in Atlanta. She's a lot like the millions of others who stood in line to make their voice heard in this election except for one thing: Ann Nixon Cooper is 106 years old.

"She was born just a generation past slavery; a time when there were no cars on the road or planes in the sky; when someone like her couldn't vote for two reasons — because she was a woman and because of the color of her skin.

"And tonight, I think about all that she's seen throughout her century in America — the heartache and the hope; the struggle and the progress; the times we were told that we can't, and the people who pressed on with that American creed: Yes we can."

A massive crowd fills Grant Park in Chicago to participate in Barack Obama's victory celebration.